CHAUCER STUDIES XI

INTRODUCTION TO CHAUCERIAN ENGLISH

CHAUCER STUDIES

ISSN 0261-9822

INTRODUCTION
TO
CHAUCERIAN ENGLISH

ARTHUR O. SANDVED

D. S. BREWER

© A. O. Sandved 1985

First published 1985 by D. S. Brewer
240 Hills Road, Cambridge
an imprint of Boydell & Brewer Ltd
PO Box 9, Woodbridge, Suffolk IP12 3DF
and of Boydell & Brewer Inc.
Wolfeboro, New Hampshire 03894-2069, USA

Reprinted 1988

British Library Cataloguing in Publication Data
Sandved, Arthur O.
  Introduction to Chaucerian English.—(Chaucer
  studies, ISSN 0261–9822; XI)
  I. English language—Middle English, 1100–1500
  —Grammar   I. Title   II. Series
  427′.02   PE531
  ISBN 0-85991-180-2

Library of Congress Cataloging in Publication Data
Sandved, Arthur O.
  Introduction to Chaucerian English.

  (Chaucer studies; 11)
  Includes indexes.
    1. Chaucer, Geoffrey, d. 1400–Language.   2. English
  language—Middle English, 1100–1500—Phonology.
  3. English language—Middle English, 1100–1500—
  Morphology.   I. Title.   II. Series.
  PR1940.s26   1985   821′.1   85–3834
  ISBN 0-85991-180-2

Photoset in Great Britain by
Rowland Phototypesetting Ltd, Bury St Edmunds, Suffolk
Printed and bound by Short Run Press Ltd,
Exeter, Devon

Contents

Preface

There is fairly general agreement that the modern reader's appreciation of Chaucer's writings can be enhanced by providing the reader with guides to 'Chaucerian background'—literary, historical, and cultural. And students of Chaucer are fortunate in having at their disposal a large number of books covering various aspects of Chaucerian background. One field which is less well covered is Chaucer's language. It is true that certain aspects of Chaucer's syntax and lexis have been dealt with in fairly recent years. But other sub-categories of Chaucerian English, such as phonology and morphology, deserve more attention than they have normally received. The absence of readily available guides to these aspects of Chaucer's English has placed the linguistically oriented student at a considerable disadvantage compared with his more literary minded colleague. But the latter is also in need of a more detailed and more reliable guide to Chaucerian English than the somewhat scant notes often included in editions of Chaucerian texts. The present book is intended to meet this need. It is largely limited to Chaucerian phonology and morphology since, as has already been suggested, the need seems to be greatest in these fields.

The book is primarily intended for students at undergraduate university level. A certain familiarity with the rudiments of linguistics is presupposed, but the technical terminology has been kept at a minimum.

I should like to express my gratitude to the people who have helped me in the shaping of this book. Firstly, I am grateful to those students at the University of Oslo who were exposed to a trial version of the typescript, and who helped to remove some of the weaknesses of the earliest draft. Secondly, I want to thank those of my colleagues who have taken time to read the typescript and to comment on it. In particular I should like to record my gratitude to Professor Trygve Heltveit and Professor Eva Sivertsen for encouragement and for valuable comments. I owe a special debt of gratitude to Mr Michael Benskin, who has read the whole of the typescript and who has made a number of useful suggestions. For the weaknesses which no doubt remain I am alone responsible.

Oslo, December 1983. A.O.S.

TO RUTH
in affection and gratitude

Abbreviations

adj	adjective
C	consonant
fem	feminine
gen	genitive
ind	indicative
inf	infinitive
masc	masculine
ME	Middle English
MS(S)	manuscript(s)
OE	Old English
OF	Old French
p	person
p(p)	page(s)
part	participle
pl	plural
pron	pronoun
RP	Received Pronunciation
sg	singular
subj	subjunctive
v	verb

For Chaucer's works the following abbreviations are used:

Anel	*Anelida and Arcite*
Astr	*A Treatise on the Astrolabe*
BD	*The Book of the Duchess*
Bo	*Boece*
CkT	*The Cook's Tale*
ClT	*The Clerk's Tale*
CT	*The Canterbury Tales*
CYT	*The Canon's Yeoman's Tale*
FranklT	*The Franklin's Tale*

INTRODUCTION

In an introductory book on Chaucerian English of a scope like that of the present one, only a limited number of aspects of Chaucer's language can be considered. This means that the writer has been confronted with the problem of deciding what aspects to deal with, and more basically, of finding a guiding principle for making this decision. The guiding principle that has been adopted in this book is agreement or disagreement between Chaucerian English and present-day English.[1] Generally speaking, our discussion will be focused on points where Chaucerian English differs from present-day English.

The first difference between the two types of English that should be noted is of a general nature, viz. the difference in the status of the two types of English within the language communities in which each of them is/was used. Present-day *written* English is an unrivalled *standard* language, considered as a model worthy of imitation not only by speakers of RP, but by virtually all writers of English throughout the English-speaking world. Chaucer's written English was not a standard language in the sense that it was a model imitated by all writers of English in the second half of the fourteenth century. Indeed, there is no evidence that it was used outside the London area. On the other hand, there is evidence that slightly different types of written English were acceptable, not just in London, but even in the much more limited linguistic circle of the court. The truth is that in Chaucer's day there was no national standard written language in England. But the movement which eventually resulted in such a standard may in a sense be said to have begun in the second half of the fourteenth century. In relatively recent times four different types of late ME have been identified which may be said to represent 'initial stages' in the movement towards a national standard written language. Chaucer's English was one of these. It is sometimes referred to as 'Type III'.[2]

1. By 'present-day English' in this context is meant the type of spoken English usually referred to as 'Received Pronunciation' (RP), and the type of written standard English regularly used by speakers of RP.
2. On this see M. L. Samuels, 'Some Applications of Middle English Dialectology', *English Studies* 44 (1963), pp. 84 ff.; and Arthur O. Sandved, 'Prolegomena to a renewed study of the rise of Standard English' in *So meny people longages and tonges*, ed. by Michael Benskin and M. L. Samuels, pp. 38–40.

It is a general characteristic of written standards that they have reached an advanced stage of 'homogeneity' or 'stability', by which is meant here that there are relatively few points of usage which are unsettled. In this respect, too, there is a marked difference between Chaucer's language and present-day standard written English. In the latter there are, relatively speaking, very few points of unsettled usage. Some are found for instance in the tense formation of verbs, where quite a few verbs have regular and irregular forms existing side by side, e.g. *(a)waked* and *(a)woken*, *burned* and *burnt*, *dwelled* and *dwelt*, etc. Chaucer's English is very different in this respect. For one thing the larger 'type' of written English to which Chaucer's English belongs—'Type III'—is much more heterogeneous than present-day written English. If Chaucer's English is compared with other examples of Type III, considerable differences of detail emerge. This is one reason why this kind of English is referred to as a 'type' rather than a 'standard'. But the linguistic heterogeneity also emerges if Chaucer's language is considered by itself, i.e. without any comparison with other Type III writings. The number of unsettled points of usage in Chaucer's English is much larger than in present-day Standard English. In very many cases Chaucer has two or more alternative forms existing side by side. Thus, to mention just a couple of examples here, the past singular of the verb SEE appears as *saw*, *sawe*, *saugh*, *sawgh*, *seigh*, *sigh*, *sy*, and *say*. The third person singular present indicative of the verb HOLD appears as *holdeth* and as *halt*. Usually in such cases one of the variants is the normal or majority form, the other(s) being more or less 'abnormal'. Such a flexible state of the language offers a great many advantages to a poet, and Chaucer exploited these advantages to the full. As might be expected, when minority variants are used, they often occur in rhyme. Indeed Chaucer felt free to use in rhyme not only forms which were rare in contemporary London English, but even forms which must have been alien to it.

'London English' in the second half of the fourteenth century must in itself have been a very heterogeneous linguistic entity. The language spoken and written in London had undergone dramatic and rapid changes in the period from about the middle of the fourteenth century till the 1380s and 1390s.[3] These changes were mainly due to large-scale immigration from other parts of the country, chiefly the Midlands. London in the second half of the fourteenth century was, therefore, very much of a linguistic melting-pot, and the linguistic heterogeneity of Chaucer's written English is doubtless in no small degree a reflection of a similar heterogeneity found in the spoken language of contemporary London.

So far we have been using the terms 'Chaucer's English' and 'Chaucer's language' as if this were an easily retrievable and identifiable entity. This is by no means the case, however. With the possible exception of one prose text, the *Equatorie of the Planetis* (and even this is doubtful), no autograph MS of any Chaucerian text is known to be extant. Chaucer's works, then, have reached us only after having gone through a process of copying and recopying, the number of intermediate stages between Chaucer's original and the extant MSS being unknown. Anyone who is at all familiar with medieval scribes' tendency to 'translate' the text they were copying into their own type of language will realise how dangerous it is to draw conclusions about 'Chaucer's language'—in

---

3. On this see M. L. Samuels, *Linguistic Evolution*, pp. 166–70.

the strict sense of 'the language written by the poet and civil servant Geoffrey Chaucer'—from the data observable in extant MSS of established Chaucerian texts. The fact that the *Canterbury Tales* have come down to us—wholly or in part—in more than eighty different MSS suggests something about the magnitude of this problem. A simple example may be illustrative: The *Parliament of Fowls* is known to us in fourteen different MSS. In one standard edition of Chaucer's work, line 436 appears as

Al be she nevere of love me behette

For *Al be* a number of MSS have *Although*;
for *she* one MS has *it that he*, another has *it she*, and two others have *that she*;
for *nevere of love me* one MS has *me neuere of loue*, another has *of loue she me neuere*;
for *behette* one MS has *beheette*.[4]

How is one to decide what Chaucer's original line looked like?

As regards the *Canterbury Tales*, readers will get a good idea of the difficulties that face the student of 'Chaucer's language' by consulting the eight volumes of John M. Manly and Edith Rickert's *The Text of the Canterbury Tales*.

Students should realise, then, that the text found in a modern edition of a Chaucerian work is not 'what Chaucer wrote' in the strictest possible sense, but usually a text which has been established through a normal process of editing. Such a process involves among other things such matters as choices between different MS readings, emendations of corrupt readings, corrections of scribal mistakes, etc.

The text on which the present book is based is F. N. Robinson, *The Works of Geoffrey Chaucer* Second Edition (1957). The *Romaunt of the Rose*, which is included in Robinson's edition, but 'of which Chaucer's authorship is altogether doubtful' (Robinson, p.xxix), has not been laid under contribution. For the editorial principles adopted in Robinson's edition the reader is referred to the Introduction, pp.xxxvi–xliv.

It follows from what has just been said that the language described in this book and referred to as 'Chaucerian English', is not 'Chaucer's language' in the strict sense defined above, but the language found in one particular edition of works which by common consent are included in the Chaucer canon,[5] in a text which may be assumed to be reasonably close to 'what Chaucer wrote'.

4. According to the textual notes given in D. S. Brewer's edition of the poem, p. 96.
5. As has already been suggested, Robinson's edition contains some poems, the authorship of which is doubtful. Mention has already been made of the *Romaunt of the Rose*. A few short poems of doubtful authorship appear on pp. 540–43 of the second edition. On the other hand, the *Equatorie of the Planetis* is not included in Robinson's edition.

PART I

PHONOLOGY

CHAPTER 1

Preliminary Remarks

Apart from the obvious reason that a study of Chaucerian phonology adds to our general knowledge of the history of the English language, there are more specific reasons why a study of Chaucerian phonology is worthwhile. For one thing such a study serves the practical purpose of enabling us to read Chaucer's poetry aloud with something like his own pronunciation. Many people will agree that Chaucer's poetry can be enjoyed properly only if it is read aloud. It is poetry for the ear. It should not be forgotten that Chaucer wrote his poems about a century before Caxton set up the first printing press in England. It is commonly accepted that Chaucer presented his poems to his contemporaries by reading them aloud to a (court) audience. There is therefore a sense in which Chaucer's poems may be said to have been written for the purpose of being read aloud.

Secondly, a study of Chaucerian phonology is a prerequisite for a full appreciation of Chaucer's use of rhyme. Rhyme is a very important feature of Chaucer's verse. All his works in verse are rhymed, and, as we shall see later, Chaucer seems to have been very particular about his rhymes. For anything like a full understanding and a proper appreciation of Chaucer's use of rhyme a fairly extensive knowledge of his phonology is needed. A good example of this is provided by the rhymes in which the name of the city of Troy is one of the rhyme words in *Troilus and Criseyde*. In that poem the name *Troye* occurs in rhyme in 31 places, and with one single exception it always rhymes with *joye*. Whether this is due to an attempt on Chaucer's part to create 'a sort of refrain expressive of joy or sorrow as the occasion may arise', as one scholar has suggested,[1] or simply to the scarcity of words rhyming with *Troye* in Chaucerian English, as suggested by another scholar,[2]—can only be decided on the basis of a sound knowledge of Chaucerian phonology—in this case a knowledge of the functional load of the phoneme /ɔɪ/ in Chaucerian English.

The vexed question of the rhythm of Chaucer's verse, which has been the

---

1. Michio Masui, *The Structure of Chaucer's Rime Words*, §142.
2. Norman Davis, 'Chaucer and Fourteenth-Century English', *Writers and their Background Geoffrey Chaucer*, ed. by Derek Brewer, pp. 58–84. See pp. 66–67.

subject of a lengthy debate among critics and philologists, provides another example of a problem which cannot be solved without extensive knowledge of at least certain aspects of Chaucerian phonology.

What kind of evidence is available for the study of the phonological system of Chaucerian English—a type of English, it should be remembered, which was current in London six centuries ago? Is it at all possible to determine Chaucer's pronunciation? The answer depends on what is meant by 'Chaucer's pronunciation'. Certain features of his pronunciation, e.g. his intonation, are irretrievably lost to us. Nor can we ever be absolutely sure about the exact phonetic realisation of his phonemes. In our study of Chaucerian phonology, therefore, it would be wise to pursue less ambitious aims. We might for instance limit ourselves to establishing the inventory of (segmental) phonemes. On the other hand, we are interested in Chaucer's rhymes, and this has important consequences for our approach to Chaucer's sound system. Rhymes depend on the phonemic/phonetic categories used by the rhymer and perceived by his audience. Commonly these categories correspond to phonemes as defined by the modern analyst, but some such categories can be expected to be subphonemic. A rhyme, by definition, involves the repetition of an identical (sequence of) sound(s). Since the phonetic realisation of a given phoneme is partly dependent on the sequence of sounds in which it occurs, it follows that a study of rhymes will of necessity take us beyond the phonemic to the sub-phonemic level. Thus, to take an example from present-day English, the rhyme *had:bad* contains not just one and the same vowel phoneme /æ:/, but also the same characteristic 'long' allophone of /æ:/ used before the voiced aveolar plosive /d/. In this respect the *had:bad* rhyme differs from e.g. *hat:bat*, in which the phonetic realisation of /æ:/ will be the 'short' allophone used before unvoiced plosives. (Cf. the discussion of Chaucerian /y:/ and /æ:/ below, pp. 18–20 and 22–23.)

In view of the difficulties involved in this dual approach: (a) pursuing the less ambitious aim of establishing the inventory of phonemes, and (b) studying rhymes, which takes us beyond the phonemic level, there is something to be said for abandoning the phonemic frame-work of our study of Chaucerian sounds and adopting a less rigorous approach. However, there are good practical and pedagogical reasons for studying Chaucer's sound system in terms of phonemes and allophones, etc., and in this book these practical and pedagogical considerations have been given precedence. Our discussion of Chaucer's phonology will not go very far beyond establishing the probable inventory of segmental phonemes.

What evidence is available, then, for a study of Chaucerian phonology thus delimited? The most important types of evidence are *spelling*, *rhymes*, and *comparison with earlier and later stages of English* (and also with other languages, e.g. French).

Spelling is to be used with great caution, because spelling soon becomes traditional and hence may be unphonemic. It is certain that Chaucerian spelling is not phonemic, i.e. there is no one-to-one correspondence between phonemes and written symbols, graphemes, in Chaucerian English. This makes it necessary to draw any conclusions warily. Still, spelling is an important type of evidence. Certain features of the spelling may at least help us to form hypotheses, which may then be tested by means of additional evidence. Thus, to take only a couple of examples, when we find in Chaucerian English an apparently unsystematic, haphazard, alternation between *ay* and *ey* in words like *payne/peyne, pray/prey, way/wey*, etc., it is fairly safe to take this as an indication that *ay* and *ey* are two different symbols used to represent one and the same phoneme (or possibly sequence of phonemes). This in its turn is at least a suggestion that in Chaucerian English there was no phonemic opposition between, say an /aɪ/- and an /eɪ/- diphthong. Or, to take another example, when Chaucer consistently spells the word DELIGHT without *gh* (the normal spellings are *delit(e)* and *delyt(e)*), we may take this at least as an indication that the phonemic structure of the second syllable of the word was different from that of, say LIGHT, which is consistently spelt *light/lyght*. The unetymological present-day English spelling of DELIGHT was introduced in the sixteenth century. It was made possible by the loss of the palatal fricative in words like LIGHT, which we assume was still pronounced in Chaucerian English. (Cf. the discussion of Chaucer's consonant system below, pp. 30–32.)

In using *rhymes* as evidence in a phonological analysis of Chaucer's English we are making certain assumptions about the exactness of his rhymes. This is a complex question, which cannot be discussed in detail here. At this stage the reader will have to take it on trust that there is considerable evidence to suggest that Chaucer was very careful with his rhymes. Indeed, there is evidence that some of his rhymes may have been 'over-true', in the sense that he avoided rhyming words the vowels of which were probably (slightly) different allophones of one and the same vowel phoneme. (On this see below, pp. 22–23.) On the other hand, there can be little doubt that some rhymes in Chaucer are imperfect. However, it is a fairly safe assumption that the vast majority of Chaucer's rhymes are true rhymes, and may therefore be said to constitute an important type of evidence for a study of Chaucerian phonology.

Comparison with earlier and particularly later stages of English is perhaps an even more important type of evidence. For earlier stages of the language we have again to rely heavily on such evidence as spelling and rhymes (though rhymes are not used with anything like the same frequency in pre-Chaucerian as in post-Chaucerian literature). For later stages of English a most important type of evidence may be added, viz. the descriptions of English pronunciation provided by early grammarians, spelling reformers and orthoepists. These begin to appear from about the middle of the sixteenth century, i.e. about 150 years after Chaucer's death. Comparison with present-day English pronunciation also often gives valuable insight into Chaucerian phonology.

A good example of how rhymes and comparison with present-day English (and also earlier English) can be used in combination is provided by certain words ending in *-oon*. (The same words also serve to illustrate the inadequacy of spelling as evidence. Cf. above.) There are a number of words which in Chaucerian English are always spelt *-o(o)n* (with or without a final *-e*). The analyst's first assumption would naturally be that the words in question contain the same sequence of phonemes. A closer look at the words, however, reveals that they fall into different classes. Words like *boon* (BONE), *goon* (inf. of GO), *stoon* (STONE) normally rhyme with each other, but not with *doon* (inf. of DO), *moon* (MOON), *soon* (SOON), the latter forming another group of words which normally rhyme only with each other.[3] This in itself is sufficient to throw doubt on the initial assumption that all words in question contain one and the same

3. There are a few exceptions to this rule, to which we shall return later. See p. 23.

sequence of phonemes. Comparison with present-day English suggests very strongly that two different vowel phonemes are involved here. It will be seen that the present-day English reflexes of *boon*, *goon*, and *stoon* are pronounced with the diphthong /əʊ/, whereas the reflexes of *doon*, *moon*, and *soon* are all pronounced with /uː/. And comparison with Old English clinches the matter. The OE etyma of *boon*, *goon*, and *stoon* are *bān*, *gān*, and *stān* respectively, (the ‾ indicates a long vowel), whereas those of *doon*, *moon*, and *soon* are *dōn*, *mōna*, and *sōna*. More examples could be given, but enough has perhaps been said to give the reader an idea about the most important sources of knowledge about Chaucerian phonology that are available to us, and about how they may be tapped.

CHAPTER 2

Short Vowels

Chaucer's system of short vowels in stressed syllables seems to have been this:

/ɪ/ close front	/ʊ/ close back
/e/ half-close front	/o/ half-close back
	/a/ front or central

This should be compared with the corresponding RP system:

/ɪ/	/ʊ/
/e/	
/æ/	
	/ʌ/
	/ɒ/

The most notable difference between the Chaucerian system and that found in RP is in the number of phonemes. In Chaucerian English there were five short vowels in stressed syllables, whereas present-day English has six. The new phoneme /ʌ/ came into being through a process known as 'phonemic split'. Chaucerian /ʊ/ split in two, as it were, and appears sometimes as present-day English /ʊ/, as in FULL, PULL (the /ʊ/ has been retained chiefly after labial consonants), but usually as present-day English /ʌ/, as in CUT, LOVE.

In accordance with our aim, set out above, p. 10, we shall limit our discussion of the phonetic realisation of these phonemes to a few words about the quality of Chaucer's /a/. This has been much debated. The normal reflex of this vowel in present-day English is the open front vowel /æ/, which is generally held to be a more front variety than Chaucerian /a/ (hence the difference in transcription). In certain phonemic contexts, e.g. after /w-/ and before /-l/, Chaucer probably had a more retracted allophone. Note that in such cases the present-day English reflex is not the usual /æ/, but some other (generally back) vowel: WALK, WAS; ALL, FALL.

THE SPELLING OF SHORT VOWELS

It will be necessary to say a few words about the way(s) in which these phonemes are usually spelt. /a/, /e/, and /o/ are unproblematic in that they are spelt *a*, *e*, and *o* respectively.

/ɪ/ is spelt either *i* or *y*. The latter spelling is preferred by some scribes in the neighbourhood of minims, i.e. letters consisting of downward strokes, to avoid confusion. Since *i* is not always 'dotted' in medieval MSS (the mark used is actually not a dot, but a hairline stroke), and since the stroke may easily be misplaced, series of minims are likely to give difficulty to a reader. The classic example to illustrate this difficulty is the noun *minimum*, which consists of no fewer than 15 consecutive minims.

Examples:
hir, his, lippes, pilgrimage, but also *pilgrymage*;
knyght, hym (39 times in Gen Prol, as opposed to 6 instances of *him*),
myghte, nyght(e).

/ʊ/ is spelt either *u* or *o*. The distribution of *u* and *o* for /ʊ/ is similar to that of *i* and *y* for /ɪ/ mentioned above. The letter *o* is often used in the neighbourhood of minims, again for the sake of clarity: *cut, but, ful, lust, purs, tubbe; come, love* (*v* in medial position is generally written *u*, i.e. consists of two minims, in medieval MSS), *monk, month* (but generally *muche(l)*). As will be seen, some of these *o*-spellings (of what was in Chaucerian English /ʊ/) have been retained in present-day English.

From what has been said about spelling so far, it will appear that the symbol *o* in Chaucerian texts is ambiguous, in that it may represent at least two different phonemes (we shall see later that it may in fact represent more). The student will therefore need some guidance in order to be able to interpret the symbol correctly. A rough and ready rule which holds good in many cases is that *o* represents Chaucerian /o/ if present-day English has /ɒ/, as in *cok, fox, God, John, knokke, on*; but Chaucerian /ʊ/ if present-day English has /ʌ/ or /ʊ/, as in *som, sonne, wonder, wonne* (past part. of WIN); *womman*.

In cases like *word, world, worm, wortes* (NPT 3221), *worthy*, etc., where *o* is preceded by *w-* and followed by *-r*, the *o* may be assumed to represent /ʊ/ in Chaucerian English; /wʊrd/, /wʊrld/, etc.

It is also probable that *o* in *wol* (= WILL) represents /ʊ/ rather than /o/.

In addition to the short vowels set out above, Chaucer had a vowel /ə/, which only occurred in unstressed or weakly stressed syllables. It should be noted that although the occurrence of /ə/ is limited to unstressed or weakly stressed syllables, the latter very often also have a 'full' vowel. The /ə/ is especially common in inflectional suffixes, but was probably also used in some derivational affixes, though judging from the spelling, the latter seem on the whole to have had 'full' vowels.

The 'weak' vowel /ə/ is usually represented in spelling by *e*:

accorded, asked, tellen, wordes;
mayden, lovere,
under.

In a relatively few cases *i* (sometimes *y*) is used:

Nowelis (flood), carpenteris, ellis (more often: *else*).

Of particular interest is the use of the inflectional suffix *-is* (*-es*) in rhymes with the verb *is*. There are several such rhymes in Chaucer, e.g.

NPT: *beryis*   : *mery is* 2965–66,
      clerkis   : *clerk is* 3235–36,
      swevenys   : *sweven is* 2921–22.

As can be seen from the following two rhymes in PF, the spelling of the inflectional suffix is not always 'adjusted':

      bowes   : *inow is* (183–85),
      here is   : *speres* (57–59).

A similary exceptional rhyme occurs in Gen Prol involving another inflectional syllable, viz.

      savith   : *Significavit* (661–2),

but, as will be seen, this is not a perfect rhyme.

Note also Gen Prol

      (for the) nonys   : *noon ys* (523–24),

where again an unusual spelling has been used, though this time not in an inflectional syllable. (The normal spelling is *nones*.)

   It is sometimes suggested that spellings like *clerkis* indicate a pronunciation /ɪs/ rather than /əs/. While it is not inconceivable that Chaucer in reciting his poems may have used a pronunciation /ɪs/ rather than /əs/ to make the rhymes as good as possible in these cases, it would be unwise to draw hasty, general conclusions on this basis about the phonetic realisation of the 'weak' /ə/-phoneme in unstressed syllables in Chaucerian English. That the variation between *e* and *i(y)* in unstressed syllables was a matter of spelling rather than pronunciation in Chaucerian English is suggested by the way the prefix BE- as in BEFALL, BEFORE, BEGIN, BESET, etc., is spelt in different Chaucerian texts. In the CT this prefix is usually spelt *bi-*, occasionally *by-*, while in PF, whose textual history is different from that of CT, it is spelt *be-* 22 times and *by-* five times.

FINAL *-e*

Before we leave the 'weak' phoneme /ə/, a few words must be said about the pronunciation of final *-e* in Chaucer's language. The problem of final *-e* in Chaucer has caused a great deal of controversy among scholars. This is not the place to rehearse the arguments for and against the pronunciation of final -*e*[4], but a few points may be noted. It is generally accepted that the 'full' vowels of unstressed syllables in OE had been reduced to the 'weak' vowel /ə/ in ME. This is reflected in ME spelling, where the reflexes of words like OE *lufu* (LOVE), *nama* (NAME), *sunne* (SUN) and *rīdan* (RIDE) appear as *love, name, sonne,* and *riden* (later with loss of final -*n, ride*). The difficulty is to decide when such final -*e*'s ceased to be pronounced. The prevailing view today is that final -*e* was disappearing in London English about Chaucer's time, and that Chaucer pronounced it or omitted it as his metre required. There is a certain amount of evidence in Chaucerian texts that final -*e* was pronounced sometimes at least. Thus in Gen Prol there is the rhyme *Rome:to me* (671–2); In MillT we find *pa me:blame* (3709–10); in Tr, Book 1, 2, (4), 5 *Troye* rhymes with (*joie* and) *fro ye* (FROM YOU); in SqT, 675–6 *yowthe* (YOUTH) rhymes with *allow the* (ALLOW YOU); and in CYT, 1204–5 we find *tyme* rhyming with *by me*.

Chaucer's rhymes also provide evidence of a 'negative' kind which suggests that final -*e* was usually pronounced in rhyme. 'Negative evidence' here means absence of rhymes which might have been expected to occur if final -*e* had been dropped. As E. Talbot Donaldson pointed out in one of the articles referred to in footnote 4,[5] if the final -*e* in words like *chivalrye* and *lye* (LIE) was no longer pronounced, then one would expect to find such words rhyming with words ending in -*y*. Yet with one single exception such rhymes do not occur in Chaucer. And it is to be noted that by accepting such rhymes Chaucer would have increased his stock of rhymes of this kind very considerably. He would in that case have been free to include for instance all the words formed with the suffix -*ly*. The exception is 'The Tale of Sir Thopas' where *chivalry* rhymes with the name *Sir Gy* (899–902). But 'The Tale of Sir Thopas' is a burlesque on popular minstrel poetry, and there can be little doubt that this rhyme constitutes one of the devices used by Chaucer in 'Sir Thopas' to poke fun at this type of poetry.

Evidence of this kind (the above examples are by no means exhaustive) is sufficiently strong to make most linguistic historians believe that final -*e* in Chaucer's poems was sometimes pronounced. The generally accepted rule is that final -*e* should be pronounced

(a) at the end of the line, and
(b) within the line, if the metre requires it.

---

4. The interested reader is referred to the debate between James G. Southworth and E. Talbot Donaldson in the *Publications of the Modern Language Association of America*, vols. 62 (1947), 63 (1948), and 64 (1949).
5. 'Chaucer's Final -E', *PMLA*, 63 (1948), 1122–3.

CHAPTER 3

Long Vowels

The system of long vowels in Chaucerian English probably contained the following phonemes:

/i:/ close front   /u:/ close back
/e:/ half-close front   /o:/ half-close back
/æ:/ half-open front   /ɔ:/ half-open back
                    /a:/ open central (or front)

Again this should be compared with present-day English:

/i:/   /u:/
            /ɜ:/   /ɔ:/
                                    /ɑ:/

While the differences between Chaucerian English and present-day English in the system of short vowels are relatively small, those in the system of long vowels are very marked indeed. A mere glance at Chaucer's system and that found in present-day English will reveal some of these differences. For one thing the number of phonemes has been reduced. The present-day English system contains only five as opposed to Chaucer's seven. Chaucerian English has no fewer than three (possibly even four, see below) long front vowels as opposed to only one in present-day English.

But the differences between Chaucerian English and present-day English in the system of long vowels are by no means limited to the number of units in the two systems. Between Chaucer and present-day English there was a complete 'reshuffling' of the long vowels. It will be seen that both Chaucerian English and present-day English have, for instance, a long close front /i:/ and a long close back /u:/, but this does not mean that present-day English /i:/ and /u:/ are the normal reflexes of Chaucerian /i:/ and /u:/ respectively. To put this differently, words which in Chaucerian English were pronounced with a long /i:/ are not normally pronounced with a long /i:/ today, and the same applies to /u:/.

17

All the long vowels in Chaucerian English have undergone radical changes since the end of the fourteenth century. These changes are generally referred to as the Great Vowel-Shift. Briefly, the Great Vowel-Shift may be summarised like this: All long vowel phonemes were raised one step, and the two close vowel phonemes /i:/ and /u:/, which could not be further raised, were diphthongised. This can be set out in a diagram:

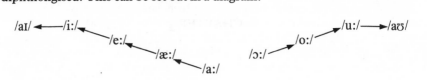

Through later changes

/i:/ and /e:/	(from Chaucerian /e:/ and /æ:/ respectively) have merged and appear as /i:/ in present-day English,
/æ:/	(from Chaucerian /a:/) has been diphthongised and appears as /eɪ/ in present-day English,
/o:/	(from Chaucerian /ɔ:/) has also been diphthongised and appears as /əʊ/ in present-day English.

The changes collectively referred to as the Great Vowel-Shift go a long way towards explaining the discrepancies between spelling and pronunciation that can be observed if English is compared with, for instance, Continental languages. The Great Vowel-Shift thus provides a historical explanation of, for example, the facts that

ride, is pronounced /raɪd/ in present-day English, but /ri:də/ in Mod. Norwegian;

side, is pronounced /saɪd/ in present-day English, but /si:də/ in Mod. Norwegian;

se(e), is pronounced /si:/ in present-day English, but /se:/ in Mod. Norwegian;

dame, is pronounced /deɪm/ in present-day English, but /da:mə/ in Mod. Norwegian.

More will be said about spelling and pronunciation later. Before we turn to that something must be said about certain problematic points in the system of long vowels in Chaucerian English.

SOME PROBLEMS IN THE SYSTEM OF LONG VOWELS

The Long Close Front Rounded /y:/

A relatively large part of the vocabulary of fourteenth century English consisted of French loan-words, some of which were fairly recent acquisitions. One characteristic difference between the vowel systems of Chaucerian English and French was the presence in the latter of a long close front rounded vowel /y:/. Now what happened when French words containing this /y:/, such as *virtue*, *accuse*, *rude*, etc., were borrowed into English? What normally happens when words are borrowed from a foreign language is that the sound structure of the loan-words is 'adjusted' to that of the receiving language. The vowels and consonants of the donor language are replaced by the nearest equivalents in the receiving language. The problem in connection with /y:/ is whether or not the 'adjustment' of /y:/ had taken place in Chaucer's language (and by 'Chaucer's language' here is meant the spoken English of the circles in which Chaucer, the court poet, moved). In normal linguistic circumstances one would assume that it had. But 'linguistic circumstances' were not absolutely normal in the circles in which Chaucer moved. It should not be forgotten that French was not only well known, but also *used* in court circles at this time. Chaucer's contemporary, Gower, composed poems in French, which were read by people with whom Chaucer was in constant contact. It is not unlikely that in these circles the loan-words in question were pronounced with the French /y:/. Indeed it has been commonly assumed that the /y:/ was in fact still pronounced in the French way by upper-class speakers, while speakers among whom knowledge of French was less extensive are assumed to have substituted the nearest English equivalent for it.

What would the nearest native equivalent be? *A priori* one would think that among the long vowels there are two plausible candidates, viz.

/i:/,   which—like /y:/—is close and front, but—unlike /y:/—not rounded, and

/u:/,   which is close and rounded, but not front.

Among the diphthongs (cf. below, pp. 25–27), however, there is an even stronger candidate, viz.

/ɪʊ/,   which combines the features 'closeness', 'rounding' and 'frontness' in that its starting point is close and front and the glide ends as a rounded (though back) vowel.

The native sounds which eventually did replace the French /v:/ were in the majority of cases /ju(:)/, which is clearly a reflex of Chaucerian /ɪʊ/, e.g. *virtue*, *accuse*. Sometimes /u:/ is found in present-day English, e.g. *rude*.

In accordance with the aim stated above, p. 10, our primary concern is to try to determine the phonemic status of the sound in the phonological system of Chaucerian English. Two possibilities immediately suggest themselves: Either /y:/ had not been 'integrated into' the native phonological system, and existed as a 'foreign' element restricted to French loan-words. In this case one would expect to find /y:/ rhyming only with itself in Chaucerian English—always assuming that Chaucer's rhymes are true rhymes. Or the sound had been replaced by a native equivalent, say the diphthong /ɪʊ/. In this case one would expect to find French loanwords containing original /y:/ rhyming with native words in /ɪʊ/ such as *new*, *spew*. This sounds simple: all one has to do is to study the rhymes in which original French /y:/ takes part. If /y:/ is found to rhyme only with itself, it can apparently be given status as a separate independent phoneme. If it is found to rhyme with native /ɪʊ/, it will have merged with the latter sound. In actual fact, with a single exception the sound rhymes only with itself in Chaucer's poems.[6]

6. The exception is the rhyme *aventure:honoure*, which occurs in *The Complaint of Venus*, 22–23. (Now, *honoure* is of course also a French loan-word, but its second vowel may safely be assumed to have been phonemically identical with native /u:/. The two are frequently paired in rhymes. This is of interest because it serves to corroborate the assumption made above that native /u:/ is a plausible candidate for replacing French /y:/.)

However, it would be rash on the basis of this evidence to draw the conclusion that original French /y:/ and native /ɪʊ/ were two different phonemes. There is the possibility that original French /y:/ may have been pronounced with a diphthong which was phonetically similar to, but not identical with native /ɪʊ/. But if so, the two sounds would satisfy the usual requirements for two allophones to be brought together as members of one and the same phoneme, viz. (a) non-contrastive distribution (/ɪʊ/ from /y:/ in French loan-words only, native /ɪʊ/ in all other cases), and (b) phonetic similarity. The absence of rhymes with French /y:/ and native /ɪʊ/ in Chaucer's poems *may* be explained by assuming (a) that Chaucer had a good ear for phonetic differences (he probably did), and (b) that he was very particular about his rhymes (he almost certainly was). We shall see later that a similar state of things seems to obtain in the case of long /æ:/, where Chaucer seems to have avoided rhyming two sounds which were probably allophones of one and the same phoneme. (See pp. 22–23.)

The safest position to take, then, is to admit that the phonemic status of original French /y:/ is uncertain in Chaucerian English. But since a choice has to be made, in phonemic transcription for instance, we shall use the symbol /ɪʊ/, thereby suggesting possible phonemic (though not necessarily *phonetic*) identity with native /ɪʊ/, with which—as we have seen—French /y:/ eventually merged in most cases.

The Long 'e'-Sounds

The two long vowels /e:/ and /æ:/ represent a problematic point in Chaucerian phonology. In an introductory book like this nothing like an exhaustive treatment can be attempted. Once again we shall have to content ourselves with considerably less than 'the whole truth'. It is indeed unlikely that 'the whole truth' about Chaucer's /e:/ and /æ:/ will ever be known.

The first thing that the student should note is that there are in fact two vowel phonemes involved here. The reason why this needs to be emphasised is that no consistent graphemic distinction is made between them.[7] The situation, therefore, is to some extent parallel with that which involves the two back vowels /o:/ and /ɔ:/.[8] It was pointed out above that /o:/ and /ɔ:/ have normally yielded two different phonemes in present-day English, viz. /u:/ and /əʊ/ (see p. 12). In cases of normal sound development it is possible, therefore, to determine the value of a Chaucerian *oo* by 'working back' from the present-day English reflex of the word in question. The /e:/ /æ:/ problem is more difficult because the two sounds have normally merged in present-day English.[9] Thus *bene* (BEAN) (MillT 3772 and NPT 2814) and *been* (BEEN) (NPT 3125) both appear as /bi:n/ today. (The latter, of course, also has an alternative /bɪn/.) That the two sounds were kept apart in Chaucerian English, however, is quite clear.

---

7. In some MSS of the CT there seems to be a certain tendency for /e:/ to be spelt *-eeCe* in some cases, while /æ:/ is more often spelt *-eeC* or *-eCe* (*C* represents any consonant). Note e.g. that in Gen Prol a distinction is made between *heed* (HEAD) (lines 201, 293, 455, 551, 666, 782) and *heede* (HEED) (line 303). The three *deed*-spellings at Gen Prol 148, Gen Prol 781, and NPT 2901 all represent /æ:/, while *deede* at MillT 3591 represents /e:/.
8. Cf. above, pp. 11–12, and below, pp. 23–24.
9. In some cases (particularly before an alveolar stop) /æ:/ was shortened and appears in present-day English as /e/, e.g. in DEAD, HEAD, RED.

A stanza from one of Chaucer's poems can be used to show this. The rhyme scheme of the 'Antistrophe' of *Anelida and Arcite* is *aab aab bab*. The third stanza runs like this:

1 And shal I preye, and weyve womanhede?
2 Nay! rather deth then do so foul a dede! .
3 And axe merci, gilteles,—what nede?
4 And yf I pleyne what lyf that I lede,
5 Yow rekketh not; that knowe I, out of drede;
6 And if that I to yow myne othes bede
7 For myn excuse, a skorn shal be my mede.
8 Your chere floureth, but it wol not sede;
9 Ful longe agoon I oghte have taken hede.

A study of the history of the above rhyme words in the light of what is generally known about sound development between OE and ME reveals that the rhyme words in lines 3, 6, 7 and 9—*and only these*—are words the OE etyma of which would not yield /æ:/ in Chaucerian English. These words must therefore have had /e:/. The remainder are words which would normally have /æ:/, or in some cases, one might expect to find either /æ:/ or /e:/. In other words, the stanza seems to have the rhymes

-/æ:/
-/æ:/
-/e:/
-/æ:/   i.e. we have the expected
-/æ:/   rhyme scheme *aab aab bab*;
-/e:/
-/e:/
-/æ:/
-/e:/

and the rhyme words can all be said to contain vowels which one would expect them to have in a Chaucerian text.

From what has been said so far it may be gathered that the spellings *ee* and *e* (when used for a long vowel) may represent either /e:/ or /æ:/ depending on the history of the word in which they appear. For our purpose we can divide the words in question into three groups:

(a) Those which always have /e:/.
Examples: *be, he, me, she, we; been, deep, mete* v. (MEET), *seke* (SEEK).
(b) Those which always have /æ:/.
Examples: *breed* (BREAD), *de(e)d, dede* (DEAD), *deeth* (DEATH), *dreem* (DREAM), *he(e)d* (HEAD), *re(e)d, rede* (RED).
(c) Those which can have either /e:/ or /æ:/. A study of Chaucer's rhymes reveals that there are some words which rhyme sometimes with /e:/-words and sometimes with /æ:/-words. Thus, to take only a couple of examples: In MillT line 3591 *deede* (DEED) rhymes with *speede* v. (SPEED), which had the half-close vowel /e:/, but in PF line 82 the same word *dede* rhymes with *dede* (DEAD) (line 79), which had the half-open

21

/æ:/. In MillT, line 3825 *strete* (STREET) rhymes with *grete* (GREAT), which had /æ:/, but in CkT, line 4384 it rhymes with *meete* (MEET), which had /e:/.

The fact that some words rhyme with both /e:/-words and /æ:/-words is easily accounted for. In the vast majority of cases it is due to dialectal variation. A word like DEED, for instance, had different vowels in different OE dialects. In West Saxon the word was pronounced with /æ:/, while in Anglian and Kentish it was pronounced /de:d/. And the reflexes of these alternants continued to exist in ME times as regional variants. The two variants, at least of some of the words in question, were probably current in London at this time. Cf. what was said above, p. 4 about immigration into London. In any case it is quite clear that Chaucer knew of such variants and exploited them in his rhymes.

From what has been said so far one may come to think that the correct identification of /e:/ and /æ:/ in Chaucerian texts requires a knowledge of the history of the individual words in question. But that is not so, at least not in the majority of cases. The point is that after Chaucer but before the two sounds merged, they came to be distinguished *graphemically*. The half-open /æ:/ came to be written *ea*, while /e:/ was generally written *ee*, sometimes *e*. This distinction was carried out with great consistency, which means that the correct value of a Chaucerian *ee* can normally be determined from the *spelling* of the present-day English reflex of the word in question. If this spelling is *ea*, Chaucer may be assumed to have had /æ:/. Note how the present-day English reflexes of the words used as examples above, p. 21, are spelt. There are some notable exceptions to this rule: *stepe* Gen Prol 753 (STEEP) had /æ:/, while *se(e)* (SEA) seems always to have had /e:/, to mention only two of the exceptions.

Before we leave the problem of /e:/ and /æ:/ in Chaucer, a few words must be added concerning an interesting fact about Chaucer's rhymes on long 'e'-vowels. Chaucer's long /æ:/ is a phoneme in which several OE phonemes have merged. Some /æ:/-words in Chaucerian English are reflexes of words which in OE had a diphthong /æ:ə/. This is the case with most of the words of group (b) above (p. 21). A further example of the same group of words is *bete* v. (BEAT), which goes back to an OE *bēatan*. These words, of course, regularly occur in rhymes with words of the same category. Another OE source of Chaucerian /æ:/ is OE /æ:/, e.g. *swete* v. (SWEAT), the OE etymon of which is *swǣtan*. Chaucerian /æ:/-words of this second category are relatively frequently rhymed both with /æ:/-words and with /e:/-words. (In other words, many of these are words belonging to group (c) above, p. 21.) Again, of course, they regularly rhyme with words of the same category as they themselves belong to. A third source of long /æ:/ is OE *short* /e/, which was lengthened to /æ:/ in open syllables. (An open syllable can be roughly defined as one which ends in a vowel sound.) An example of this is *ete(n)* (EAT) (from OE *etan*), which was disyllabic before the loss of final /ə(n)/, with the syllable division before the /t/. Now the interesting thing is that with very few exceptions Chaucer avoids rhyming *ete*-words with /æ:/-words of other categories. They nearly always rhyme only with themselves. Does this mean that the reflex of OE short /e/ in open syllables had not yet merged phonemically with /æ:/ from other sources? It is quite clear that in the later (standard) spoken language lengthened /e/ did merge with /æ:/ from other sources. The question then is, when did this merger occur? The probable answer is that the phonemic merger took place when the phonetic context in which the lengthening of /e/ developed, was no longer recognisable, i.e. when the syllable in which /e/ occurred was no longer open.[10] This happened when final /ə/ in words like *ete* was dropped.

It will now be seen that the problem of the phonemic status of lengthened /e/ in Chaucerian English is somewhat complex: If it is true—as is generally believed—that final /ə/ was disappearing in Chaucer's day, this means that the merger of lengthened /e/ and /æ:/ may have taken place in Chaucer's English. On the other hand, we have assumed that final /ə/ was retained *in rhyme* (cf. above, pp. 15–16); but if this is correct, the phonemic merger of lengthened /e/ and /æ:/ had not taken place *in rhymed position*. Here again, as in the case of French /y:/, the safest position to take is probably to admit that the phonemic status of lengthened /e/ in Chaucerian English is uncertain. But in any case it is interesting to note that Chaucer fairly consistently avoided rhyming the reflex of short OE /e/ in open syllables with /æ:/ from other sources. At least two conclusions may be drawn from this fact: Firstly that there must have been a phonetic difference between [æ:] in *ete*-words and other kinds of /æ:/ which was sufficiently marked for Chaucer to have noticed it. And secondly that Chaucer seems to have taken great care over his rhymes.

The Long 'o'-Sounds

We have already touched on the problem of Chaucer's long /o:/ and /ɔ:/. (See above, pp. 11–12.) For this reason, and also because this problem is in many ways parallel with that of /e:/ and /æ:/, not much need be said about it at this point. Here again, then, there are two vowel phonemes which are not distinguished graphemically. In the case of /o:/ and /ɔ:/, however, the two can usually be identified without much difficulty, since—unlike /e:/ and /æ:/—they have not merged in present-day English. Chaucerian /ɔ:/ has normally yielded /əʊ/ in present-day English, while /o:/ generally continues as either /u:/ (e.g. *food*), or /ʊ/ (*foot*), or /ʌ/ (*blood*).

As we have already seen, Chaucer usually keeps /o:/ and /ɔ:/ apart in rhyme. But here again, as in the case of the two *e*-sounds, there are some exceptions (though not so many in the case of /o:/ and /ɔ:/). Thus the verb DO, *do(o)*, *don*, *doon(e)* (infinitive or participle), usually rhymes with /o:/ words, e.g. with (*ther*) *to* Gen Prol 500, MerchT 1460; *sho* WBT 707, MerchT 1554; *soone* BD 689. But not uncommonly it also rhymes with /ɔ:/-words, e.g. with *so(o)* BD 29, 150, KnT 1195, Tr 1.828; *goon* BD 188, 194, KnT 2964; *wo* BD 1191, Tr 1.828. Another example is provided by the word ALSO, which normally rhymes with /ɔ:/-words, but occasionally with /o:/-words; e.g. with /ɔ:/ *foo* Gen Prol 64; (*y*)*go* Gen Prol 285, MillT 3631; *wo* NPT 2937; with /o:/ (*ther*) *to* FranklT 797, HF 1756. The probable explanation is again that there were alternative pronunciations of the words in question, and that Chaucer felt free to exploit these for the purpose of rhyme, even though he himself may not have used these alternatives in his own pronunciation.

Note finally yet another parallelism between *e*-sounds and *o*-sounds in Chaucer: We have seen that Chaucer generally avoids rhyming /æ:/ from OE short *e* with /æ:/ from other sources. Similarly he also normally avoids rhyming

---

10. On this see E. J. Dobson, 'Middle English Lengthening in Open Syllables', *Transactions of the Philological Society* 1962, 124–148.

the reflex of OE short /o/ in open syllables, with /ɔː/ from other sources. There is an interesting example of this in the fourth stanza of Book V of *Troilus and Criseyde*:

1 This Troilus, withouten reed or loore,
2 As man that hath his joies ek forlore,
3 Was waytyng on his lady evere more
4 As she that was the sothfast crop and more
5 Of al his lust or joies herebifore.
6 But Troilus, now far-wel al thi joie,
7 For shaltow nevere sen hire eft in Troie!

The rhyme scheme is *ababb cc*. The rhyme words in lines 1 and 3, i.e. the a-rhymes have /ɔː/ from OE long /aː/, while those in lines 2, 4, and 5, i.e. the b-rhymes, have the reflex of OE short /o/ in open syllables. (The word *more* at the end of line 4 is a noun meaning 'root', from an OE *more*, *moru*.)

THE SPELLING OF LONG VOWELS

/iː/   is generally spelt *i* or *y*, as for the short /ɪ/.

/eː/   is most often spelt *e* or *ee*, occasionally *ie*
       (e.g. *agrief:meschief* NPT, 2893–94).

/æː/   is most often spelt *e* or *ee*. In other words no consistent distinction is made in the spelling between /eː/ and /æː/. (But see above, p. 20, footnote 7.) On how to decide whether *e(e)* represents /eː/ or /æː/ see above, p. 22.

/aː/   is usually spelt *a*, occasionally *aa* (e.g. *estaat:debaat* MillT, 3229–30).

/ɔː/   is generally spelt *o* or *oo*.

/oː/   is spelt in the same way as /ɔː/, i.e. *o* or *oo*.
       As has been pointed out already, Chaucerian *oo* or *o* (when used for a long vowel) can generally be assumed to represent /ɔː/ if the present-day English reflex of the word in question has /əʊ/, otherwise /oː/.
       Thus *boon* was /bɔːn/, cf. present-day English /bəʊn/, BONE,
       stoon was /stɔːn/, cf. present-day English /stəʊn/, STONE.
       While on the other hand
       goos was /goːs/, cf. present-day English /guːs/, GOOSE,
       good was /goːd/, cf. present-day English /gʊd/, GOOD,
       blood was /bloːd/, cf. present-day English /blʌd/, BLOOD,
       brother was /broːðər/, cf. present-day English /brʌðə/ BROTHER.

/uː/   is generally spelt *ou* or *ow*. It should be noted that the spelling *u* is not used for /uː/. The spelling *u* is used for short /ʊ/ (cf. above) and also for original French /yː/, i.e. Chaucerian /ɪʊ/, as in *mesure*, *Nature*, *vertu*. etc.

CHAPTER 4

Diphthongs

Chaucerian English probably had the following six diphthongs:

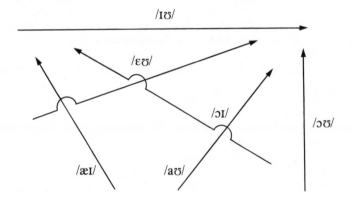

As usual we compare this with the system found in RP:

Closing diphthongs in RP

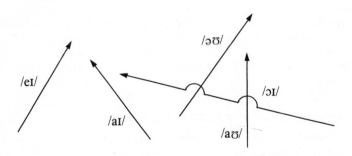

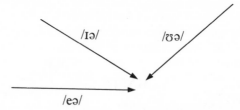

Here again as in the system of long vowels the differences between Chaucerian English and present-day English are quite marked. For one thing the inventory of diphthongs is larger in present-day English (eight as opposed to six). But again the difference is not just one of number of items in the system. Here too there has been a 'reshuffling', similar to, though less marked than that seen in the system of long vowels. That the radical changes which took place in the system of long vowels should have repercussions on the system of diphthongs is indeed only to be expected. The two systems are after all not watertight compartments. On the contrary, there has been free traffic between them: some of Chaucer's long vowels appear as diphthongs in present-day English, and some of his diphthongs appear as long monophthongs.

For the purpose of comparison between the two systems the diphthongs may be classified into three sub-groups on the basis of the end-point of the glide:

	/ɪ/-*glides*	/ə/-*glides*	/ʊ/-*glides*
Chaucerian English	/ɔɪ/ /æɪ/		/ɪʊ/ /ɛʊ/ /aʊ/ /ɔʊ/
Present-day English	/ɔɪ/ /eɪ/ /aɪ/	/ɪə/ /eə/ /ʊə/	/əʊ/ /aʊ/

It will be seen that whereas present-day English has three /ɪ/-glides, Chaucer had only two, there being no distinction like that between /eɪ/ and /aɪ/ in Chaucerian English.

/ɔɪ/, which had a small functional load in Chaucerian English (it occurs mostly in some French loan-words), continues as /ɔɪ/ today: ANOINT, POINT.

/æɪ/ normally appears as /eɪ/ today: DAY, GREY, MAY. Present-day English /aɪ/ comes from Chaucerian /iː/ (cf. above, p. 18).

Chaucerian English had no fewer than four /ʊ/-glides, while present-day English has only two:

/ɪʊ/
/ɛʊ/ } generally appear as /juː/, /uː/ today: NEW, TRUE, FEW.
/aʊ/ generally appears as /ɔː/ today: LAW, TAUGHT.
/ɔʊ/ generally appears as /əʊ/ today: KNOW, SOUL.

26

But it should be noted that present-day English /əʊ/ is very often a reflex of Chaucerian long /ɔ:/, as in STONE, HOME (cf. above, p. 12).

Present-day English /aʊ/ comes from Chaucerian /u:/ (see p. 18).

A final, most remarkable difference is the absence from Chaucerian English of any /ə/-glide. /ə/-glides, or centring diphthongs, arose after the loss of final and pre-consonantal /r/ in RP.

The two diphthongs /ɪʊ/ and /ɛʊ/ are somewhat problematic. For one thing they have merged in present-day English, as we have seen. Secondly, they are not distinguished in spelling, cf. below. Yet Chaucer seems to have kept them carefully apart. Now, unlike what was the case with the long '*e*'-sounds and '*o*'-sounds discussed above, it is not possible to set up a simple rule for the correct identification of the two sounds. They cannot be correctly identified without some knowledge of the etymology of the words in which they appear. This might seem to make matters extremely complicated. But the problem takes on a minor proportion when one considers the functional load of /ɛʊ/. This is very small, so small in fact that it is quite possible to learn the words individually. The most important words in question are: *fewe* (FEW), *lewed* (LEWD 'unlearned'), *shewe* v, (SHOW), *beautee* (BEAUTY). For a discussion of the status of /ɪʊ/ in relation to original French /y:/ see above, pp. 18–20.

THE SPELLING OF DIPHTHONGS

/æɪ/   is normally spelt *ai, ay, ei*, or *ey*.

/ɔɪ/   is normally spelt *oi* or *oy*.

/aʊ/   is normally spelt *au* or *aw*.

/ɪʊ/   is normally spelt *ew*; in French loanwords usually *u: newe* (NEW), *hewe* (HUE); *vertu, Nature*.

/ɛʊ/   is normally spelt *ew*. For examples see above.

/ɔʊ/   is normally spelt *ou, ow*, or *o: soule* (SOUL), *knowe, broghte* (BROUGHT).

CHAPTER 5

Pronunciation Rules

It will have appeared from our discussion of the Chaucerian vowel-system that a number of spellings are ambiguous. It may therefore be useful to sum up the most important of these spellings and to give simple rules for the pronunciation of ambiguous vowel-symbols. It must be emphasised that only those points which are likely to give difficulty to the beginner are mentioned, and that the rules given are no more than rough and ready guide-lines, to which there are numerous exceptions.

a may represent the short vowel /a/ or the long vowel /a:/.
  (i) It should be pronounced /a/ if present-day English has /æ/.
       Examples: *bak* (BACK), *man, sadde* (SAD).
  (ii) It should be pronounced /a:/ if present-day English has /eɪ/.
       Examples: *name, shake, tale.*
e may represent the short vowel /e/, the long vowel /e:/ or the long vowel /æ:/.
  (i) It should be pronounced /e/ if present-day English has /e/.
       Examples: *men, sende, wente.*
  (ii) It should be pronounced /e:/ if present-day English has an /i:/ which is not represented in spelling by *ea.*
       Examples: *be, grene* (GREEN), *he, me, sene* (SEEN).
  (iii) It should be pronounced /æ:/ if present-day English has /i:/ represented in spelling by *ea.*
       Examples: *ete* (EAT), *pes* (PEACE), *rede* v. (READ), *teche* (TEACH).
       In quite a few cases present-day English has /e/ spelt *ea: brede* (BREAD), *ded(e)* (DEAD), *hede* (HEAD). Note that *there, were,* and *where* normally had /æ:/.
ee always represents a long vowel, which is either /e:/ or /æ:/.
       To decide which, use the rules given above under *e,* (ii) and (iii).
ew always represents a diphthong, which is either /ɪʊ/ or /ɛʊ/. The former should be used in all cases except in a relatively few words, the most important of which are *beautee, fewe, lewed, shewe.*
i may represent the short vowel /ɪ/ or the long vowel /i:/.

(i)   It should be pronounced /ɪ/ if present-day English has /ɪ/.
Examples: *milk, silk, spille, wille*.

(ii)   It should be pronounced /iː/ if present-day English has /aɪ/.
Examples: *delit(e)* (DELIGHT), *I*, *lik* (LIKE).

o may represent a short vowel, which is either /ɔ/ or /ʊ/; a long vowel, which is either /ɔː/ or /oː/, or (in a few cases) a diphthong, /ɔʊ/.

(i)   It should be pronounced /ɔ/ if present-day English has /ɒ/.
Examples: *God, on, oxe*.

(ii)   It should be pronounced /ʊ/ if present-day English has /ʌ/.
Examples: *sonne*, (SUN), *yronne* (past part. of RUN),
          bigonne (BEGUN), *love*.

(iii) It should be pronounced /ɔː/ if present-day English has /əʊ/.
Examples: *go, old, so, wo* (WOE).

(iv) It should be pronounced /oː/ if present-day English has /uː/.
Examples: *do, scole* (SCHOOL), *to*.
In some cases present-day English has a short vowel which has developed from a long post-Chaucerian /uː/, e.g. in *brother, (an)other*.

(v)   It should be pronounced /ɔʊ/ before *-ght(e)*.
Examples: *broghte, noght* (NOUGHT, NOT), *roghte* (= 'cared'), *thoghte, wroght*.

oo always represents a long vowel, which is either /oː/ or /ɔː/.
To decide which, use the rules given above under *o* (iii) and (iv).

ou ⎫
ow ⎭ may represent the long vowel /uː/ or the diphthong /ɔʊ/.

(i)   They should be pronounced /uː/ if present-day English has /aʊ/.
Examples: *foul, hous; how, now*.

(ii)   They should be pronounced /ɔʊ/ if present-day English has /əʊ/ or /ɔː/ (generally before *-ght*).
Examples: *although, soule* (SOUL), *oughte, thoughte; growe, knowe*.

u may represent the short vowel /ʊ/ or the diphthong /ɪʊ/.

(i)   It should be pronounced /ʊ/ if present-day English has /ʊ/ or /ʌ/.
Examples: *ful, pulle; but, under, unto, up(on)*.

(ii)   It should be pronounced /ɪʊ/ in French loan-words.
Present-day English generally has /ju(ː)/ or /uː/.
Examples: *entuned, rude, vertu*.

y may represent the short vowel /ɪ/ or the long vowel /iː/.
Rule as for *i* above.

CHAPTER 6

Consonants

The consonant system of Chaucerian English is generally thought to have included the following phonemes:

/p b			t d	tʃ	dʒ		k g	
	f v	θ ð	s z	ʃ			x	h
m			n					
			l					
w			r			j/		

If this is compared with the system found in RP today it will be seen that there are relatively few differences:

/p b			t d	tʃ	dʒ		k g	
	f v	θ ð	s z	ʃ	ʒ			h
m			n				ŋ	
			l					
w			r			j/		

Since we are mainly concerned with the differences between Chaucerian English and present-day English, and since the two consonant systems are relatively similar, it follows that our discussion at this point can be brief. The following points should be noted:

1. There are certain differences in the *inventory of phonemes*:

(a) It will be seen that there is a velar fricative /x/ in Chaucerian English. This phoneme is generally considered to have had two main allophones, both of them normally spelt *gh*, viz.

[ç] a palatal variant, sometimes referred to as the German *ich*-sound, which occurred after front vowels, e.g. *bright* [brɪçt], *knyght* [knɪçt], *heigh* [hæɪç] (HIGH); and

[x] a velar variant, sometimes referred to as the German *ach*-sound,

which occurred after back vowels, e.g. *brought* [brɔʊxt], *plough* [plu:x], *thought* [əʊʊxt].

The above analysis is the traditional one. There is, however, an alternative analysis, which accords well with the available evidence, and which has much to recommend it, viz. that the glottal fricative [h] should be grouped together with·[ç] and [x] as allophones of one and the same phoneme. The two sounds [ç] and [x] are regarded as allophones of /x/ because they satisfy the usual requirements (a) non-contrastive distribution ([ç] only after front vowels and [x] only after back vowels), and (b) phonetic similarity (palatal fricative and velar fricative). But [h] is in complementary distribution with [ç] and [x] ([h] only occurs initially and [ç] and [x] never occur initially). And the phonetic similarity between the palatal and the velar fricatives [ç] and [x], on the one hand and the glottal fricative [h] on the other, would seem to be sufficiently great for them all to be grouped together as allophones of one and the same phoneme.

Note that the alternative analysis would 'bring the Chaucerian system closer to that of present-day English' in the sense that the 'additional' fricative consonant /x/ in Chaucerian English would be removed. The difference between Chaucerian English and present-day English on this point would then be moved from the phonemic to the sub-phonemic level of analysis.

(b) There is another difference between Chaucerian English and present-day English in the sub-system of fricatives, viz. the absence from the former of the voiced palato-alveolar fricative /ʒ/. This phoneme arose through a fusion of /z/ and a following /ɪ/ or /j/, as in *vision*, /vɪzjʊn/ˌ/vɪʒən/. Note, therefore, that in Chaucerian texts words like *vision* are to be pronounced with the cluster [-zj-], or [-zɪ-].

In this connection it might also be pointed out that the corresponding unvoiced fricative /ʃ/, which was part of the Chaucerian consonant inventory, had a somewhat smaller functional load than /ʃ/ has in RP, because since Chaucer's day there has been a similar fusion of /s/ plus a following /ɪ/ or /j/ in cases like e.g. *complexioun*, /-sɪu:n/ˌ/-ʃ(ə)n/, *confessioun*, /kon'fesɪu:n/ˌ/kən'feʃn/.

(c) A third difference which concerns the inventory of consonants is the absence from Chaucerian English of the velar nasal phoneme /ŋ/. The sound [ŋ] existed in Chaucerian English only as an allophone of /n/ before the velar stops /k/ and /g/, as in *synge* [sɪŋgə], *thynke* [əɪŋkə]. /ŋ/ acquired phonemic status only after final /g/ in words like *sing* had been lost. Loss of final /g/ in e.g. *sing* meant that /ŋ/ was now in minimal contrast with /n/, as in *sing:sin*.

2. There are certain differences between Chaucerian English and RP in *the distribution of consonant phonemes*. Again it is in the sub-system of fricatives that we find some of the most important differences.

(a) A number of function words (grammatical words) in present-day English end in a voiced fricative, e.g. *as, has, his, was, of, with*. At an earlier stage in the history of English the final fricative in these words was unvoiced. These are words that often occur under weak stress, and the voicing of the final consonant is apparently related to absence of stress. The voicing is generally thought to have occurred after Chaucer's time. In Chaucerian texts there are a number of rhymes which clearly suggest that the final consonant was unvoiced at least sometimes. Thus we find

> *is* rhyming with e.g. *amys* (AMISS), *blis* (BLISS), *this*, *ywis* (from OE *gewis*, cf. German *gewiss*; = 'certainly'), all of which must have had a final unvoiced /s/;
> *was* rhyming with e.g. *bras* (BRASS), *cas* (CASE), *glas* (GLASS), *gras* (GRASS), *Nicholas*, *solas* (SOLACE), which also had a final /s/.

Rhyme-words are of course normally stressed, so that what these rhymes suggest is that the unvoiced /s/ was used in final position under primary stress. They do not tell us anything about whether or not the fricative was unvoiced in unstressed position. That the words in question at some stage have had 'strong forms' with an unvoiced final fricative and 'weak forms' with a voiced one is very probable. And it is of course possible that this stage had already been reached in Chaucer's day. Some scholars think that it had. In an introductory course like this the problem is of little consequence, and students may safely use the unvoiced fricative in all cases.

It should be noted that the final /s/ in inflectional syllables of words like *bones*, *pigges*, *wordes*, etc., has had the same history as /s/ in function words like *as*, *is*, etc. That is to say, in Chaucerian English this inflectional syllable is generally thought to have been pronounced /-əs/. The final /s/ was later voiced, yielding /-əz/, and then loss of unstressed /ə/ gave /bəʊnz/, /pɪgz/, /wɜːdz/.

(b) Another group of function words in present-day English have a voiced initial fricative /ð/: *the*, *this*, *these*, *that*, *those*, *than*, *then*, *there*, etc. Here again a voicing of an originally unvoiced fricative has taken place, and once more under weak stress. In the case of these words, however, there is a certain amount of evidence that the voicing is pre-Chaucerian. Many scholars believe that these words had initial /ð/ in Chaucerian English.

3. Certain *consonant clusters* which are unacceptable today were still tolerated in Chaucerian English. Thus in initial position we find /kn-/, /gn-/ and /wr-/ as in *knyght* /knɪxt/, *knowe* /knɔʊə/, *gnof* /gnof/ (MillT, 3188) (= 'ill-mannered person', 'churl'), *write* /wriːtə/.

Similarly, though non-initial /-lf, -lk, -lm/ are not unacceptable clusters in RP (*self*, *milk*, *elm*), in a number of cases a written *l* is silent before *f*, *k*, and *m* in present-day English. In Chaucerian English the *l* was sounded in all such clusters: *half*, /half/, *folk*, /folk/, *palmeres* /palmərs/.

Note finally that *r* was sounded in pre-consonantal (and also in final) position: *March* /martʃ/, *or* /or/.

PART II

MORPHOLOGY

CHAPTER 7

Preliminary Remarks

In our discussion of Chaucerian morphology we shall again confine ourselves to some of the most important differences between Chaucerian English and present-day English. The theoretical frame-work of our discussion and the terminology used is that found in chapters 2 and 3 of P. Christophersen and A. O. Sandved, *An Advanced English Grammar* (1969).

Chaucerian morphology differs from that of present-day English in various ways. There are differences in the inventory of morphemes. That there are differences in the inventory of base morphemes is so obvious that no exemplification is needed. In the following discussion relatively little will be said about base morphemes. The discussion will concentrate very largely on *inflectional suffixes* (and other types of inflection), though we shall also have a few words to say about *prefixes* and *derivational suffixes*.

Differences in morpheme inventory between Chaucerian English and present-day English are not limited to base morphemes. The inventory of affixes is not the same in the two varieties of English, as will be demonstrated below. And in cases where the same affix is found in both varieties, there are quite frequently differences both in semantic range and in distribution. Thus, to give just a few examples, there is a semantic difference between the derivational suffix -STER in Chaucerian English and in present-day English in that nouns formed by means of -*stere* in Chaucer denote female agents (*beggestere* = 'female beggar'), whereas nouns formed with -*ster* in present-day English do not (*trickster*). There are differences in 'productiveness', i.e. the freedom with which affixes may be used to form new words, as when Chaucerian -*ward* can be added e.g. to a place-name like *Canterbury* to form a word *Caunterbury-ward*. And there are differences in the range of individual bases to which a given affix may be added, so, e.g. Chaucerian -*age* can be added to bases like *cost*- and *cosin*- to form words meaning 'expense' and 'cousinship' (or, more generally, 'kinship') respectively. Many of these differences are obvious enough and will not generally be commented on. In fact the discussion of derivational affixes that follows is limited to just some of the most salient differences between the two varieties of English.

35

CHAPTER 8

Prefixes

In morphemic analysis identification of morphemes may at times be problematic because it is not always easy to ascertain the precise degree of semantic similarity between a given set of (potential) allomorphs. (A 'morpheme', it will be remembered, is sometimes defined as 'a group of allomorphs that are semantically similar and in complementary distribution'.) This problem is considerably more difficult in the case of prefixes since quite often their meanings are particularly vague. It may seem fairly obvious that a distinction should be made between, say

> *for-* (1) as in *forheed* (FOREHEAD) Gen Prol 154; *forseyde* (AFORESAID) PF 120, *forwityng* (FOREKNOWLEDGE) NPT 3243, where the meaning of *for* is something like 'before' (in space or time), and
> *for-* (2) as in *foryeve* (FORGIVE) Gen Prol 743, where no such meaning as 'before' is discernible.

But is the meaning of *for-* in *foryeve* sufficiently similar to that in, say *forlore* (= 'lost') MillT 3505, for these two instances of *for-* to be classified as the same prefix? Or, to put the question differently, how many prefixes *for-* should we acknowledge in Chaucerian English? Similarly, is *a-* in, say *arise* Gen Prol 249, in which *a-* is a reflex of the OE prefix *ā-* (OE *ārīsan*), to be regarded as a different prefix from *a-* in *athynketh* (= 'regret') MillT 3170, in which *a* is a weakened form of *of-* (OE *ofþyncan*)? Since our aim is nothing like a complete morphemic analysis of Chaucerian English, problems like these may be allowed to remain unsolved. It is of some importance, however, to realise their existence, and uncertainties like these should be kept in mind throughout the discussion which follows.

Most of the prefixes found in Chaucerian English are still in use. Among those which have since disappeared should be noted:

> *i-/y-* is a relatively common prefix in Chaucerian English. Its chief use is with past participles of verbs:
> *ydoon, yfounde, imaked, yronne.*

36

The prefix is a reflex of OE *ge-*, and is historically the same as the *ge*-prefix found in modern German (*getan, gefunden*, etc.). Although *i-/y-* is particularly frequent in the past participle, it is not limited to this form. An example of an infinitive prefixed by *y-* is found in MillT 3176: *yheere*. In a few cases we find it with other words than verbs; thus *ywis* (= 'certainly'; cf. German *gewiss*), *ylyk* (LIKE).

of-   is a relatively rare suffix, meaning 'away', used with verbs, e.g. *of-caste* ('throw away') PF 132, *of taken* PrT 665 (not hyphenated in Robinson's text).

to-   This verbal prefix was fairly common in OE and ME. Its meaning is something like 'asunder, apart, in pieces', and it is often prefixed to verbs which in themselves express separation, division and the like. As examples consider the three occurrences of it found in PF: *torent* (= 'rent to pieces'), line 432, *to-shyvered* (= 'broken into pieces'), line 493, *totorn* (= 'torn to pieces'), line 110.

an-   is used as a prefix in e.g. *anhanged* (= 'hanged') NPT 3062, 3140.

In a number of cases where a Chaucerian prefix has been retained in present-day English, there are differences in their use. As examples consider:

a-   The problem of morpheme identification discussed above is particularly difficult in the case of *a-*, which has a variety of sources. In addition to the uses of *a-* illustrated above, the following might be noted: *amorwe* Gen Prol 822 (= 'in the morning'), *a-nyght* NPT 3167, *a-nyghtes* MillT 3214 (= 'at night, in the night'); *atwynne* MillT 3589 (= 'apart, separately'). *on-* occurs in *on-lofte* (PF 683), which is a variant of *alofte* (PF 203), (= 'on high, in the air').

for-   We have already seen that there are good reasons for distinguishing between (at least) two prefixes *for-* in Chaucerian English, viz.

for- (1) with the meaning 'before' as in *forheed* (FOREHEAD); *forwityng* (FOREKNOWLEDGE), with the corresponding verb *forwoot* NPT 3234, 3248 (= 'knows in advance'). This prefix is now spelt *fore-*.

for- (2) with no such meaning as 'before'. There is one particular use of this second *for-* that should be noted, viz. the one exemplified by *forpyned* Gen Prol 205, *a forpyned goost*. In this case *for-* has an intensive force, somewhat similar to the corresponding prefix in other Germanic languages; cf. e.g. Norwegian, 'forpint', which would in fact be a good translation of *forpyned* at Gen Prol 205.
In MillT line 3120 occurs a construction which is possibly another example of this use of the prefix *for-*:
The Millere, that *for dronken* was al pale.
But in this case another analysis is possible and perhaps preferable. (The fact that *for* and *dronken* are not printed as one word is of no consequence. Spacing in ME manuscripts is notoriously difficult and hyphens in printed texts are generally editorial.) *Forpyned* in *a forpyned goost* is clearly an adjectival word, but it is not obvious that *for dronken* in the above construction is used in the same way. It should be noted that

37

the adjective *pale* is not linked to *for dronken* by *and*, which is what one would naturally have expected if both of them had been adjectivals. The alternative analysis is to take *for* in *for dronken* as a preposition used to indicate cause or reason (= 'the Miller, who was very pale for, i.e. because of, drunkenness'). But after a preposition one expects a noun or a noun-like word, not an adjective, and *dronken* cannot be taken as anything but the past participle (which may of course be used adjectivally). However, there was an idiom in Chaucerian English in which the preposition *for* could be followed by an *adjective* in substantival or semi-substantival function to denote cause or reason. An unambiguous example of this is found in Tr, Book II, line 656:

And with that thought, *for pure ashamed*, she
Gan in hire hed to pulle . . .

Here, obviously, there is no way of taking *for* as a prefix. This must be a case of causal use of the preposition *for*. On the other hand, there is at any rate one clear example of *for-dronke(n)* with intensifying prefix in Chaucer:

And sodeynly he was yslayn to-nyght,
Fordronke, as he sat on his bench upright.
(PardT 673–74).

It has been suggested, therefore, that the construction at MillT 3120 could be taken in both ways.[1] Another, similarly ambiguous construction occurs in PF:

But fynally, my spirit at the laste,
For wery of my labour al the day,
Tok reste . . .   (92–94)

Here again it is difficult to decide whether *for* serves as a prefix (*forwery* = 'exhausted') or as a preposition indicating cause, (= 'for weariness').

---

1. E.g. by Tauno F. Mustanoja in his *Middle English Syntax*, p. 382, where a more detailed discussion of this problem may be found.

CHAPTER 9

Derivational Suffixes

-e: One of the most important differences between Chaucerian English and present-day English in the system of derivational suffixes is the existence in the former of a derivational suffix -*e*, used to form adverbs from adjectives:

cleere	Gen Prol 170;	cf. the adjective *cler* PF 210,
faire	Gen Prol 94;	cf. *fair* adj. Gen Prol 154, 204, 369,
harde	MillT 3279;	cf. *hard* adj. Gen Prol 229, PF 2, 534,
loude	Gen Prol 714;	cf. *loud* adj. MillT 3332.

As has already been pointed out (p. 16), final -*e* is generally assumed to have been disappearing in London English at the time of Chaucer, which means that the existence of the adverbial suffix -*e* was a precarious one. The examples listed above are clear enough, because in all cases both the spelling and the metre suggest that a final /ə/ was pronounced. But, as also has been pointed out, Chaucer felt free to drop the final -*e* to meet metrical demands. Thus adverbial -*e* was probably dropped in e.g. *brode* Gen Prol 739; *faire* Gen Prol 124, 273, 539; *foule* PF 517; *hoote* Gen Prol 97; *loude* Gen Prol 171, 672, all of which are followed by a word beginning with a vowel or /h/. It is interesting to note that -*e* is retained in the spelling in these cases. A graphemic distinction is thus maintained between these adverbs and the corresponding adjectives *brood* Gen Prol 155, 471, 549, 553; *fair* (for references see above); *foul* Gen Prol 501, NPT 2813, 2897; *hoot* Gen Prol 626; *loud* MillT

39

3332. But such a graphemic distinction is not made consistently.

-esse: There were two suffixes *-esse* in Chaucerian English,

-esse (1) used as in present-day English to form feminine nouns like *emperesse, goddesse, prioresse*;

-esse (2) used to form abstract nouns from adjectives, where present-day English has *-ness: gentillesse, richesse*.

-nesse is a more frequently used suffix in Chaucerian English as well: *bytternesse, hevynesse, lightnesse*, etc.

-hed: used to form abstract nouns from other nouns where present-day English generally has *-hood: bretherhed*. It could also be used to form abstract nouns from adjectives: *falshede, liklihede*.

-hod is an alternative in Chaucerian English: *knyghthod* PF 549;

manhod Gen Prol 756; *wyfhod* WBT 149.

-(at)if/-(at)yf: used to form adjectives (many of which may also be used as nouns) from verbs and nouns: *hastif, inquisitif, jolif, laxatyf*. Present-day English generally has *-ive*, but note *hasty* and *jolly*,

-lich: used to form adjectives from nouns: *estatlich* Gen Prol 140. Its alternative *-ly* (which has of course developed from *-lich*) is much commoner in Chaucerian English: *estatly* Gen Prol 281, *manly, worldly, yemanly*, etc.

-liche: is the corresponding adverbial suffix, which may be added to adjectives and nouns: *roialliche* Gen Prol 378, *rudeliche* Gen Prol 734. Here again *-ly* is much more frequent: *gladly, hertely, pryvely, soothly*, etc.

-som: used to form adjectives from other adjectives, as *gladsom* NPT 2778, and from nouns, as *wlatsom* (= 'loathsome') NPT 3053. This suffix provides an illustration of a difference between Chaucerian English and present-day English mentioned above, viz. the freedom with which affixes may be combined with bases. *Wlatsom* is now obsolete. (The noun from which it is formed, *wlat* (= 'disgust'), seems to have become obsolete even before Chaucer. It does not occur as a free morpheme in Chaucerian texts.) *Gladsome* is obsolete or obsolescent today. On the other hand a number of adjectives in *-some* have been added to the language since the time of Chaucer. *Adventuresome, lonesome*, and a number of others are given by the *Oxford English Dictionary*.

-stere: It has already been pointed out (p. 35) that *-stere* in Chaucerian English was used to form feminine agent nouns:

beggestere (= 'female beggar') Gen Prol 242,

tappestere (= 'female tapster') Gen Prol 241, MillT 3336.

The corresponding masculine suffix was -er(e):
carpenter, haberdasshere, millere, outridere.

-ward: mostly used to form adverbs (toward is a preposition).
The suffix usually denotes 'direction of movement':
dounward, homward, upward; afterward. Forms in
-ward(e)s are rare in Chaucer.
The most important thing to note about this suffix is that
its freedom of occurrence is larger in Chaucerian English
than it is today. Thus in Chaucerian texts we find constructions like

fro Burdeux-ward	Gen Prol 397,
to Caunterbury-ward	Gen Prol 793,
unto the gardyn-ward	MillT 3572.

In cases like these there may be some doubt as to whether
ward should be regarded as a suffix or as a free morpheme.
(Again it should be remembered that hyphens are generally editorial.)
(The -ward which occurs in for(e)ward Gen Prol 33, 829,
848, 852 should not be confused with the suffix under
discussion. For(e)ward is here a noun meaning 'agreement' and the -ward is historically a different element.)

In the case of quite a few suffixes the most conspicuous difference between
Chaucerian English and present-day English is in the phonemic (and graphemic) structure of the suffix. Thus we have

Chaucerian:
- -aunt, /aʊnt/ as in repentaunt
- -aunce, /aʊnsə/ as in substaunce
- -ioun, /ɪ'uːn/ as in confessioun
- -our, /uːr/ as in { governour / reportour }
- -(i)tee, /(ɪ)teː/ as in { facultee / fraternitee }

corresponding to present-day English:
- -ant /ənt/
- -ance /əns/
- -ion /(ə)n/
- -or } /ə/
- -er }
- -ty /tɪ/
- -ity /ɪtɪ/

So far in this chapter we have been concerned with *prefixes*, which are all
derivational, and with derivational *suffixes*. It need hardly be pointed out that
both in Chaucerian English and in present-day English derivation may take
other forms than affixation (though *historically* suffixes have often been
involved even in words which to contemporary eyes do not seem to have any.)
To realise this it is sufficient to consider such related words as

speke	(verb)	: speche	(noun)	
synge	(verb)	: song	(noun)	
myrie	(adj.)	: myrthe	(noun)	
proude	(adj.)	: pryde	(noun).	

Since Chaucerian English and present-day English are mostly in agreement in
such cases, it may be left to the reader of Chaucerian texts to make his own
observations.
A couple of notable differences may, however, be pointed out: There is

clearly a derivational relationship, no longer existing, between the adjective *old* as in MillT 3225 and the noun *elde* MillT 3230; and similarly between the adjective *brode* (BROAD) MillT 3315, and the noun *brede* (BREADTH) in *hande-brede* (= 'hand's breadth') MillT 3811.

CHAPTER 10

Inflection

It may be regarded as a part of the grammatical meaning of inflectional suffixes that they identify the grammatical category of the words to which they are added. Thus the presence of the past tense morpheme -ED marks the form in which it occurs unambiguously as a verb. A convenient way of organising the discussion of inflectional morphemes, therefore, is to group together those inflectional suffixes which are characteristic of one and the same grammatical category, or, in other words, to take as the framework of our discussion the inflectional word-classes of the language. For Chaucerian English and for present-day English this gives us a frame-work of four inflectional classes of words: nouns, adjectives,[2] pronouns, and verbs. We shall deal with them in that order.

NOUNS

The inflection of nouns in Chaucerian English is basically the same as in present-day English, though there are a number of differences of detail. Chaucer's nouns are inflected for two grammatical categories: NUMBER, where a distinction is made between the singular (sg) and the plural (pl), and CASE, where a distinction is made between the common case and the genitive. No case distinction is generally made in the plural of nouns. In addition there are a very few traces of an old dative case.

Inflection for Number

REGULAR PLURAL FORMATION

The plural morpheme in Chaucerian English has two basic allomorphs, /əs/, spelt -es, and /s/, spelt -s. The distribution of these two is largely phonemically conditioned:

2. Some adverbs also take inflectional suffixes. See below, pp. 55–56.

43

/əs/ is used after consonants, e.g.

arm	:	armes,	book	:	bookes,
fish	:	fishes,	lond	:	londes.

/s/ is used after vowels, e.g.

herte	:	hertes,	soule	:	soules
tree	:	trees.			

IRREGULAR PLURAL FORMATION

The rule stated above may be said to be the regular plural formation, but there are a number of irregularities, the most important of which will be mentioned below.

First, there are certain *minority spelling variants* of the regular allomorphs of the plural morpheme:

/əs/ is occasionally spelt -*ys*:
   herys (HAIRS) Gen Prol 555,
   swevenys (= 'dreams') NPT 2921 (rhyming with *sweven is*).

The expected form of the noun EAR in Chaucerian English is *ere* with a final -*e*, and indeed that is the form we find, e.g. PF 519. To account for the plural form *erys* (Gen Prol 556, 589), therefore, one would have to say that the final -*e* of the base has been dropped before the addition of the plural suffix. The regular plural form (with /s/, spelt -*s*, added after a vowel) is seen in *eres* PF 500.

-*is*   is another minority spelling of /əs/:
   clerkis NPT 3235 (rhyming with *clerk is*)
   heeris (HAIRS) NPT 2904 (cf. *herys* above).

The irregular spelling -*is* is again found with the noun EAR, *eeris* NPT 2903, in rhyme with *heeris*.

Another irregular plural found in rhyme is *beryis* (BERRIES) NPT 2965, rhyming with *mery is*. In this case not only the spelling is irregular, the form is irregular also because the syllabic allomorph of the plural morpheme rather than the normal /s/ is used after a vowel.

/s/   is sometimes spelt -*z* after *t*: *servantz* Gen Prol 101, *juggementz* ClT 439, *instrumentz* MerchT 1713, 1715. This -*tz* is historically *t* plus a Latin abbreviation for -*es*, which looks like the letter *z*.

Plural in -(e)n

In some nouns the plural morpheme takes the irregular shape /ən/ or /n/, the distribution of /ən/ and /n/ being phonemically conditioned in the same way as /əs/ and /s/: /ən/ after consonants, /n/ after vowels:

oxe   :   *oxen*

In Chaucerian texts the noun EYE appears in the singular as *eye* and *ye* /iːə/ (as opposed to the *pronoun ye* /jeː/), and occasionally as *eighe* (FranklT 1036 in rhyme, Bo 5.pr.4.146 not in rhyme). The plural form is most often *eyen*, e.g.

44

Gen Prol 152, 201, 267, 625, 684, 753, but sometimes *yen* /iːən/, e.g. NPT 3161, 3305.

Some nouns have *-(e)n* plurals and *-(e)s* plurals existing side by side. The commonest are:

bee	:	*been*, e.g. Tr 4.1356
		bees, e.g. SumT 1693,
fo(o)	:	*fo(o)n*, e.g. MkT 2706, PF 103
		foos, e.g. Tr 1.1001
		foes, e.g. Pity 55 (with an 'irregular' *-es*
		spelling after a vowel, cf. below p. 47),
hose	:	*hosen*, e.g. Gen Prol 456
		hoses, e.g. MillT 3319, ParsT 420–5,
too	:	*toon*, e.g. NPT 2862
		toos, e.g. NPT 3180

A similar vacillation is found in *do(u)ghtren*, e.g. FranklT 1429: *do(u)ghtres* (e.g. NPT 3375) and *sustren* (e.g. KnT 1019): *sustres* (e.g. NPT 2867), but in these nouns there is an allomorphic variation of the base in that the syllabic structure of the base changes. The sg. forms *do(u)ghter* (e.g. ClT 168, PF 214) and *suster* (e.g. KnT 871) drop the vowel of the second syllable when the plural suffix is added.

A similar syllabic alteration is found in *brother:bretheren* Gen Prol 252 b, though in this case the *-e-* of the second syllable has been retained in the spelling. The metre suggests, however, that *bretheren* here was disyllabic. A more obvious allomorphic variation in this word is of course the vowel-change

/oː/ *brother* ›/e(ː)/*bretheren*.

Two more nouns with *-(e)n* plural and allomorphic variation of the base should be noted, viz. *child:children* and *cow:keen* (NPT 2831). In the former the base is altered in two ways, only one of which is revealed by the spelling. Not only is *-r-* inserted before pl. /ən/, but there is also a vowel change in that the sg. has a long /iː/, /tʃiːld/ cf. present-day English /tʃaɪld/), while the pl. has a short /ɪ/, /tʃɪldrən/. In the latter a long /uː/ in the sg. is replaced by a long /eː/ in the pl.

Plural by Vowel Change

In some nouns the plural is formed by a vowel change ('replacive allomorph' of the plural morpheme). The commonest nouns in question are:

foot	:	*feet*
goos	:	*gees*
man	:	*men*
tooth	:	*teeth*
womman	:	*wommen*

MOUSE, which belongs to the same group, only occurs in the sg. *mous*.

Zero Plurals

A relatively small group of nouns have no overt plural marker ('zero allomorph') in Chaucerian English. The most important zero plurals are:

Singular:			Plural:	
ca(a)s (CASE)	Gen Prol 797, MillT 3385	:	caas	Gen Prol 323
deer	FrT 1370	:	deer	FranklT 1195
folk	PF 524	:	folk	Gen Prol 12, 25
pound	CYT 674	:	pound	Gen Prol 454
sheep	NPT 2831	:	sheep	Gen Prol 496
swyn	MLT 745	:	swyn	Gen Prol 598
vers	Tr I. 399	:	vers	PF 124, 141

Neet ('cattle') (Gen Prol 597), is in the same group, but no clear example of a sg. form seems to occur in Chaucerian texts.

Again some nouns vacillate between this plural formation and the regular one, e.g.

Singular:			Plural:	
ye(e)r	Gen Prol 764, PF 475	:	yeer	Gen Prol 82, 601 MillT 3223, NPT 3117 but also
			yeres	NPT 3216
thing, thyng	Gen Prol 810, PF 20	:	thyng	MerchT 1485, but
			thynges	Gen Prol 175, 759
hors	Gen Prol 287	:	hors	Gen Prol 74, but also
			horses	ParsT 432, 434
and				
wynter	MLT 197	:	wynter	MkT 2059, but also
			wynters	Astr II, 26.20.

Plural of Nouns of More than One Syllable

Another kind of 'irregularity' has to do with the distribution of the regular allomorphs /əs/ and /s/. As noted above (p. 44) the normal distribution of these is for /əs/ to be used after consonants and /s/ after vowels. Now, in nouns of more than one syllable /s/, spelt -*s*, is often found after consonants:

frankeleyns, nacions, sessiouns;
auctours, colours, daungers, hunters;
conceils, coverchiefs, instruments, tercelets.

Indeed this phenomenon is so common that the general rule for the formation of the plural of nouns formulated above should perhaps be modified so as to account for it. However, disyllabic and polysyllabic nouns are also sometimes found with -*es* rather than -*s* in the plural. It is not always easy, or indeed possible, to decide whether this -*es* constituted a separate syllable. Metrical evidence seems to suggest that very often the -*e*- of the plural suffix of such nouns was syncopated. Consider for instance the following lines:

Of *maydenes* swiche as gonne here tymes waste	PF 283,
I can not se that *argumentes* avayle	PF 538.

In these cases the metre clearly requires a non-syllabic plural suffix in *maydenes* and *argumentes*. Similarly with *pilgrimes* Gen Prol 26; *lordynges* Gen Prol 761, 788, 828; *yeddynges* Gen Prol 237, to mention just a few more examples.

In other cases the metre requires a syllabic plural suffix, e.g.

Right as, betwixen *adamauntes* two   PF 148.

And if it is true that *-es* was pronounced as a separate syllable in *mono*syllabic nouns, then *-es* was also pronounced in *rekenynges* Gen Prol 760 and *dremynges* NPT 3090, because both these rhyme with *thynges*.

That *-es* was pronounced as a separate syllable in nouns like *corages*, *pilgrimages* is obvious. It is also very probable that the *-es* of *digestyves* and *laxatyves* NPT 2961–62 was fully pronounced because the change from unvoiced /f/ in *laxatyf* to voiced /v/ in *laxatyves* presupposes intervocalic position.[3] Note, however, that the metre seems to require a non-syllabic plural of *laxatyves* at NPT 3154.

(The spelling *-es* is sometimes used in nouns ending in a vowel or diphthong, e.g.

conyes PF 193; *dayes* Gen Prol 258, NPT 2852, 3190;
ladyes NPT 3356; *shoes* Gen Prol 457 (but *shoos* MillT 3318).

In such cases too the metre suggests that *-es* did not constitute a separate syllable. On the unusual pl. *berryis* see above, p. 44.)

Plurals with Allomorphic Base Alternation

The mention of such nouns as *half:halves* leads naturally on to another kind of irregularity in the formation of the plural of nouns in Chaucerian English, viz. nouns which take a regular plural suffix, but in which the base shows allomorphic variation between the singular and the plural. In a group of nouns the variation is between unvoiced /f/ in the singular and voiced /v/ in the plural. The following might be noted:

elf	:	*elves*
half	:	*halves*
knyf	:	*knyves*
laxatyf	:	*laxatyves*
leef (LEAF)	:	*leves*
lif, lyf	:	*lyves*
staf	:	*staves*
theef	:	*theves*
wif, wyf	:	*wyves*

In hous /huːs/:*houses* /huːzəs/ and *ooth*, /ɔːθ/(OATH):*othes* /ɔːðəs/, we have the same type of alternation (unvoiced fricative to the corresponding voiced one), though in these cases the alternation is limited to the phonemic level.

Conversely, in cases like

3. Cf. e.g. *halves* MillT 3481 and *wyves* Gen Prol 374, MillT 3154, etc., where the /v/ is clearly in intervocalic position.

bryd (BIRD)	:	*bryddes*
cok (COCK)	:	*cokkes*
ship	:	*shippes*

we have an allomorphic variation in the base which is limited to the graphemic level: a single final consonant symbol after a single vowel symbol representing a short vowel is doubled before the plural suffix is added.

Unusual or abnormal plural forms involving allomorphic variation of the base are occasionally found in rhyme. A notable example is

day : *dawes* (FranklT 1180) (in rhyme with *felawes*).

Inflection for Case

THE GENITIVE

As in present-day English the genitive inflection is very similar to the plural inflection. The genitive morpheme in Chaucerian English has two basic allomorphs, /əs/, spelt -*es*, and /s/, spelt -*s*. With the exception noted below, the distribution of these allomorphs is basically the same as that of the corresponding allomorphs of the plural morpheme, i.e.

/əs/ after consonants:

lordes Gen Prol 47, 597,	*kynges* MillT 3217
nyghtes MillT 3485,	*preestes* NPT 3314;

but with nouns of more than one syllable ending in a consonant often simply /s/, spelt -*s*: (cf. above, p. 46):
  aungels PF 356;

/s/ after vowels:
  hertes PF 128, *Noes* MillT 3518 (but also *Noees* MillT 3616)
  oxes NPT 3004, 3027.

There seems to be—at least in poetry texts—a distributional difference worth mentioning between the allomorphs of the plural suffix and those of the genitive suffix with *trisyllabic* nouns ending in a consonant. As noted above, in such nouns the /s/, -*s*, allomorph of the plural morpheme is normally used:

  frankeleyns, nacions, parisshens, sessiouns, etc.,
  achatours, etc.

The genitive suffix is different in this respect. In poetry texts the genitive suffix in this case tends to appear not as /s/, -*s*, but as /əs/, -*es*/(-*is*):

  cherubynnes, carpenteres, (carpenteris),
  Hasdrubales, senatoures (gen. sg. MLT 981, 987; gen. pl. NPT 3371)
  Valentynes.

The reason for this difference between the plural suffix and the genitive suffix seems to be rhythmical. In all cases in question the genitive is followed by a noun with primary stress on the first syllable, and Chaucer's metre, in which stressed and unstressed syllables normally alternate, would then require phrases like these to take the rhythmical form

$/x \backslash x/(x)$:[4]

cherubynnes face	Gen Prol 624,
carpenteris wyf	MillT 3343, 3850,
Hasdrubales wyf	NPT 3363,
senatoures wyf	MLT 981,
senatoures wyves	NPT 3371
Valentynes day	PF 309, 322, 386.

The general similarity between the genitive inflection and the plural inflection also extends to some of the 'irregularities' discussed under plural inflection above.

Thus the genitive suffix also has a minority spelling variant *-is*:

Nowelis	MillT 3818, 3834,
carpenteris	MillT 3343, etc.

The genitive morpheme also has a zero allomorph. As in present-day English this is found with classical names ending in *-s*, e.g.

Epicurus owene sone	Gen Prol 336,
Kenulphus sone	NPT 3111,
Venus sone	PF 351.

But in Chaucerian English it is also found occasionally with native words. Two clear examples are:

his lady grace	Gen Prol 88,
my fader soule	Gen Prol 781.

Allomorphic base alternation is found in e.g.

goos /go:s/ (common case): *goses* /go:zəs/ gen. sg. (PF 586),

and, confined to the graphemic level, in nouns like

God	:	*Goddes*	
bed	:	*beddes*	Gen Prol 293,
man	:	*mannes*	(*manes* once PF 210),
woman	:	*womannes.*	

---

4. / indicates primary stress,
   x indicates weak stress,
    \ indicates secondary stress (which here counts metrically as primary).

Genitive of Nouns in the Plural

No morphological distinction is normally made between the common case and the genitive case in the plural. An exception to this rule is formed by nouns with irregular plural formation:

wommennes NPT 3256.

Trisyllabic nouns of the type discussed above (pp. 48–49) might perhaps be said to form another exception in that the genitive plural of these nouns would normally be /əs/ for the rhythmical reasons mentioned above, while the common case plural would normally be /s/. Compare

As, whan that Nero brende the citee
Of Rome, cryden *senatoures* wyves   NPT 3370–71

where the genitive suffix in *senatoures* is clearly /əs/, with

Whiche were his sustres and his *paramours*   NPT 2867,

and with

Of which *achatours* myghte take exemple   Gen Prol 568,

where both spelling and metre show that the common case plural suffix of *paramours* and *achatours* was /s/, not /əs/.

THE DATIVE

In a relatively few cases we find in Chaucerian English remnants of a dative inflection. It takes the form of a final *-e*, and is chiefly found in nouns occurring after a preposition in what appear to have been set phrases. They tend to occur in rhymed position. Here are a few examples:

(in) honde PF 256, 545;	cf. *hond*	Gen Prol 193, 399, 841, PF 240, 372, 418.
(in) londe NPT 2879;	cf. *lond* *land*	Gen Prol 194, 400, 579, etc., NPT 2850.
(to) shipe MillT 3540;	cf. *ship*	MillT 3543, NPT 3102
(out of) towne Gen Prol 566;	cf. *toun* *town*	Gen Prol 217, 240, 478, etc., MillT 3380.
(yer by) yeere PF 236;	cf. *yeer* *yer*	Gen Prol 347, 764, PF 475, 647, 661, 664.

But at line 674 in PF, where the phrase does not occur in rhyme, we find *yer by yer*.

Note also
(fro yer to) yeere   PF 321, 411, and
(from yer to) yere   PF 23.

ADJECTIVES AND ADVERBS

While adjectives in present-day English are inflected only for degree (*old—older—oldest*), Chaucerian adjectives are inflected for three grammatical categories: DEGREE, where a distinction is made between the positive, the comparative, and the superlative, NUMBER, singular and plural, and in addition a category which, for want of a better term, may be labelled DEFINITENESS, definite and indefinite.[5]

The inventory of inflectional adjectival suffixes is this:

-e,	used to form the plural,
-e,	used to form the definite,
-er,	the comparative morpheme,
-est,	the superlative morpheme.

Inflection for Number

The plural adjective morpheme is manifested as /ə/, spelt *-e*. The plural adjective inflection in Chaucerian English is very rudimentary. It is virtually limited to monosyllabic adjectives ending in a consonant. Thus we find for instance:

Singular:		Plural:	
blak	(NPT 2861),	*blake*	(Gen Prol 557, NPT 2935, 2936),
coold	(MillT 3754),	*colde*	(NPT 3256, PF 187),
good	(Gen Prol 445),	*goode*	(Gen Prol 74, MillT 3154, NPT 3440),
long	(Gen Prol 617, MillT 3264),	*longe*	(Gen Prol 93, 591, PF 682, 692),
yong	(Gen Prol 79),	*yonge*	(Gen Prol 664, PF 278).

A distinction between sg. and pl. is sometimes kept up in writing even though the metre requires elision of the final /ə/. Compare for instance

Short was his gowne, with sleves *longe* and wyde (Gen Prol 93),

where the *-e* of *longe* is elided, with

Ful *longe* were his legges and ful lene (Gen Prol 591),

where the metre requires the pronunciation /longə/, and similarly in

. . . the *longe* nyghtes blake (PF 682, 692).

Plural monosyllabic adjectives are sometimes found without a plural marker. Thus we find for instance

5. A petrified remnant of the old CASE-inflection, the genitive plural, is found very occasionally. Thus the word *all(e)* sometimes occurs in the genitive plural as *aller, alder*; e.g. *hir aller cappe* (Gen Prol 586) (= 'the cap of all of them'), *oure aller cost* (Gen Prol 799) (= 'the expense of all of us'). The same form is found as the first element of a compound in *alderbest* (Gen Prol 710) (= 'best of all'). Cf. also *bother* in *youre bother love* (Tr 4.168) (= 'the love of both of you').

Grehoundes he hadde as *swift* as fowel in flight (Gen Prol 190),
Jolif and *glad* they wente unto hir reste (NPT 3074).

In some adjectives there seems to have been an allomorphic variation of the base in that the (indefinite) singular form had a short vowel, while the plural had the corresponding long vowel. Thus singular adjectives like *blak*, *glad*, and *smal* rhyme with words like *bak* (BACK), *adrad* ('afraid'), and *al* respectively, all of which had a short /a/ in Chaucerian English, whereas the corresponding plural forms *blake*, *glade*, and *smale* rhyme with words like *make*, *made*, and *tale*, which clearly had a long /a:/. See e.g. (with /a/) KnT 2144, BD 494, ClT 834; and (with /a:/) KnT 899, Tr 2.50, Gen Prol 329.

(A similar allomorphic variation is found in the inflection for definiteness (cf. below, p. 53), the indefinite (singular) form having a short base vowel, while the corresponding definite form had a long one.)

Adjectival bases of *more than one syllable* are not normally inflected in the plural:

Singular:	Plural:
with *blisful* stevene (NPT 3197),	thise *blisful* briddes (NPT 3201),
so *litel* space (Gen Prol 87),	the *litel* conyes (PF 193),
in *hooly* writ (Gen Prol 739),	hunters ben nat *hooly* men (Gen Prol 178).

A number of adjectives have a *base* ending in /ə/, *-e*. These are often reflexes of adjectives which had a final *-e* in OE. No number distinction is made in the case of these adjectives. Here are a few examples:

Singular:	Plural:
a *grene* mede (PF 184),	the *grene* leves (PF 352),
ful *blithe* and glad	if that they *blithe* were
was every wyght (Gen Prol 846),	(Tr. 3.1682)
a *clene* sheep (Gen Prol 504),	*clene* maydenes (LGW G 282),
she was *wylde*	*wilde* beestes (MkT 2173).
and yong (MillT 3225),	

Other adjectives of the same type are: *deere, kene, meeke, sweete, trewe*.
    Similarly with some French loan-words:

Singular:	Plural:
a *large* man (Gen Prol 753),	hir hipes *large* (Gen Prol 472),
a *riche* gnof (MillT 3188),	robes *riche* (Gen Prol 296).

Before we leave the plural inflection of adjectives it should be noted that traces of a French plural inflection in *-s* are found sometimes in Chaucerian texts, e.g.

| places *delitables* | FranklT 899, |
| thynges *espirituels* | ParsT 780–5, 785–90. |

As will be seen from the examples, in such cases the adjective normally follows the noun it modifies—in imitation of French usage. Note that between the two examples adduced from the *Parson's Tale* there is a third occurrence of the adjective *espirituel: espiritueel freendes*, in which the adjective precedes the noun and remains uninflected.

Inflection for Definiteness

This inflection is phonemically and graphemically identical with the plural inflection of adjectives: /ə/, spelt *-e*. Like the plural inflection it is limited to monosyllabic adjectives ending in a consonant; and since it takes the same form as the plural inflection, the distinction between the definite and the indefinite is neutralised in the plural:

Indefinite:
his . . . love was *coold* (MillT 3754),
many a *fals* flatour (NPT 3325),
a *good* wif (Gen Prol 445),
as *hoot* he was . . . as (Gen Prol 626),
it was *old* (Gen Prol 174),

Definite:
the *colde* stele (MillT 3785),
O *false* mordrour (NPT 3226),
this *goode* wyf (MillT 3309),
his *hoote* love (MillT 3754),
Olde Ypocras (Gen Prol 431),
 with *-e* retained in spelling,
 though the metre requires
 elision of /ə/ before
 the vowel /ɪ/.

The above examples have been chosen in such a way as to illustrate the most important uses of the definite adjective, viz.

(a) after 'definite' determiners, such as the definite article,
 the demonstrative pronouns *this, that,*
 possessive pronouns,
(b) in forms of direct address ('vocative'),
(c) before proper names.

Again adjectives of *more than one syllable* generally remain uninflected:

In *blisful* tyme (PF 413),

the (. . .) *blisful* martir
(Gen Prol 17,770),
O *blisful* God (NPT 3050),
at *litel* prys (WBT 523),
Hir *litel* sone (ClT 681),
in *hooly* writ (Gen Prol 739),
the *hooly* . . . martir (Gen Prol 17).

Inflection for Degree (Comparison)

REGULAR COMPARISON

The inflectional *comparative* morpheme is *-er*, which has three allomorphs, /ər/, /r/, and /rə/.

/rə/, spelt *-re*, is relatively rare. It is found in a few words with stems ending in /r/ or /rə/:

	Positive:	*Comparative:*

<table>
<tr><td></td><td align="center">*Positive:*</td><td align="center">*Comparative:*</td></tr>
<tr><td></td><td align="center">*deere*</td><td align="center">*derre*</td></tr>
<tr><td>a *fer* contree (NPT 3068),</td><td></td><td align="center">the *ferre* leeve (MillT 3393).</td></tr>
</table>

(In adverbial function we find both *ferre* (Gen Prol 48), *ferrer* (Gen Prol 835), and *ferther* (Gen Prol 36).)

/r/,	spelt -*r*, is used with most bases ending in /ə/:

/r/,   spelt -*r*, is used with most bases ending in /ə/:
        a *softe* paas (MillT 3760),
        softer (MillT 3249),
/ər/,   spelt -*er*, and less often -*ere* is used elsewhere:
        bisier, brighter, fairer, lower(e), murier,
        sikerer, thikkere (PF 273).

The inflectional *superlative* morpheme is -*est*, which has the two allomorphs

/əst/, spelt -*est*, used with bases ending in a consonant or a vowel other
        than /ə/.
        Since the superlative, like the positive, may be inflected for
        'definiteness' we find forms with and without a final -*e*:
        fyneste, shorteste, yongest, goodlieste,
        (un)worthieste.
/st/,   spelt -*st* with bases ending in /ə/:
        deerest, trewest(e).

The inflectional comparative and superlative is generally limited to mono-syllabic adjectives and some disyllabic ones. Other adjectives are generally compared by means of *mo(o)re* and *mo(o)st*:

moore resonable, more blisful, the moore mury (Gen Prol 802),
moost feithful, moost precious, most worthi (PF 635),
(but cf. *(un)worthieste* above).

Even monosyllabic adjectives may take *moore* and *moost*:

moore strong (NPT 3304),
moost wise, the mooste fre.

IRREGULAR COMPARISON

The above inflection may be said to be the regular formation of the comparative and the superlative. There are a number of adjectives the comparison of which displays irregularities of various kinds. These mostly take the form of allomorphic variation of the base. Such allomorphic variation ranges from a slight graphemic alteration of the base, as when a final consonant symbol is doubled, e.g. in

gentil	—			*gentillest* (also *gentilest*),
glad	—	*gladder*	—	*gladdest,*
fer	—			*ferreste* (Gen Prol 494),

to radical changes, as when the comparative/superlative base is completely different from that used in the positive:

good — *bettre* — *best(e).*

In one group of adjectives a long vowel in the positive is replaced by the corresponding short vowel in the comparative and superlative. The change is generally reflected in the spelling by a doubling of the final consonant symbol:

greet	—	*gretter*	— *grettest(e)*,
reed (RED)	—	*redder* (NPT 2859),	
whit(e)	—	*whitter* (NPT 2863),	
hoot (HOT)	—	*hotter*	— *hottest(e).*

The same alternation between the positive and the comparative but with an additional irregularity in the superlative is seen in

late — *latter* (NPT 3205) — *last(e).*

A different kind of alternation is found in

long	—	*lenger* (Gen Prol 330, 821), (less often *longer*),	— *lengest* (PF 549),
strong	—	*strenger*	— *strengest*,
old	—	*elder*	— *eldest.*

In the adjective

leef (PardT 760) — *levere* (Gen Prol — *levest* (Tr 2.189),
lief (MillT 3501) (= 'dear') 293, MillT 3751)

a final unvoiced fricative in the positive is voiced before the comparative and superlative suffixes. This should be compared with the plural formation of such nouns as *wyf:wyves*. (See above, p. 47.)

Very irregular are:

good	—	*bettre*	— *best*
yvel	—	*worse* *werse*	— *worst* *werst*
muche(l) *many*	—	*moore* *mo(o)*	— *moost*
lytel	—	*lasse* *lesse*	— *leest.*

COMPARISON OF ADVERBS

The two categories adjectives and adverbs tend to shade into one another—in Chaucerian English even more than in present-day English. It is not clear, for instance, how *bright(e)* in the following two examples should be classified:

Hir forheed shoon as *bright* as any day   (MillT 3310),
The moone, whan it was nyght, ful *brighte* shoon   (MillT 3352).

The syntactical construction is apparently the same in both lines:

Hir forheed/The moone shoon bright(e),

but whether *bright(e)* should be taken as an adjective modifying the subject (as the spelling *bright* in line 3310 seems to suggest) or as an adverb modifying *shoon* (as the spelling *brighte* suggests) is not obvious. Quite a few of the words adduced as examples in the discussion of comparison above, may be used both as adjectives and as adverbs. Indeed, in at least one case use has been made of a form which must be classified syntactically as an adverb rather than as an adjective, viz. *lengest* at PF 549. Here are some more examples of adverbial comparatives and superlatives:

lenger (MillT 3409, NPT 3034), *louder* (NPT 3363), *murier* (NPT 3270), *best* (Gen Prol 796, PF 625), *faireste* (NPT 2869), *faynest* (PF 480), *hyest* (PF 324), *sorest* (PF 404).

No morphological distinction is made between adjectival and adverbial comparatives and superlatives. Thus *lenger* is adjectival at Gen Prol 330, but adverbial at MillT 3409, and PF 453. An exception to this rule is formed by *bet/bettre*. In the vast majority of cases *bet* is the adverbial comparative (*wel* being the corresponding positive), while *bettre* is the normal adjectival comparative:

He knew . . . everich hostiler . . .
Bet than a lazar   (Gen Prol 242),
she . . . knew it *bet* than he   (MillT 3604),
I love another . . . *bet* than thee   (MillT 3711),
And demeth yit wher he do *bet* or he   (PF 166),
A man may serven *bet* . . . In half a yer   (PF 474).

But

A *bettre* preest   (Gen Prol 524),
A *bettre* felawe   (Gen Prol 648),
Som *bettre* man   (MillT 3130),
Hir tales alle, be they *bettre* or werse   (MillT 3174).

However, the above distinction is not always maintained. *Bettre* is sometimes used in adverbial functions,

A *bettre* envyned man   (Gen Prol 342),

while *bet* may occasionally be used as an adjective:

hir condicioun is *bet* than youres   (Mel 1375).

A most unusual addition of the derivational suffix -ly after the inflectional suffix -er is seen in *murierly* (Gen Prol 714) (= 'the more merrily').

THE SUFFIXES -er AND -est USED WITH A DERIVATIONAL FUNCTION

In a very few cases the comparative and the superlative morphemes function almost as derivational rather than as inflectional suffixes in that they 'turn into adjectives' words the bases of which are not used in that function. Thus, to mention a few examples, we find

his *overeste* courtepy	(Gen Prol 290),
hir *nether* ye	(MillT 3852),
he rood the *hyndreste* of our route	(Gen Prol 622).

The base *over* is used as a preposition and as an adverb. *Hynd-* and *neth-* do not occur as free morphemes in Chaucerian English. They are found prefixed by *bi-/by-*, e.g. in *bihynde* (MillT 3239), *bynethe* (NPT 2953).

PRONOUNS

Personal Pronouns

The following diagram shows the inventory of Chaucerian personal pronouns in their most usual spellings:

		Nominative (Subject form)	Accusative (Object form)	First Genitive (Possessive adjective)	Second Genitive (Possessive pronoun)
SINGULAR	1st person	I, ich	me	my, myn, myne	myn, myne
	2nd person	thou, thow	thee, the	thy, thyn, thyne	thyn, thyne
	3rd person				
	masc.	he	hym, him	his	his
	fem.	she	hire, hir, hyre	hire, hir, hyre, here	hire, hires
	neuter	it, hit	it, hit	his	(his)?[6]
PLURAL	1st person	we	us	oure, our	oure, oures
	2nd person	ye	yow, you	youre, your	youre, youres
	3rd person	they	hem	hire, hir, here	hirs

6. I am not sure whether the second genitive of the 3rd p.sg. neuter occurs in Chaucerian texts. If it does, it no doubt takes the form *his*.

As the table reveals, the type of inflection found in the system of personal pronouns in Chaucerian English is basically the same as that seen in present-day English. There are, however, some differences, most of which will appear directly from the table. Like their present-day English counterparts, Chaucerian personal pronouns distinguish PERSON (first, second, and third persons) NUMBER (singular and plural), CASE (nominative or 'subject form', accusative or 'object form', and genitive). A further distinction is made here between what are sometimes called first and second genitives. As suggested by the alternative designations given in the table, the first genitive is generally used in adjectival function, while the second genitive is nominal. Inflection for a fourth category, GENDER, is found in the third person singular, where a distinction is made between masculine, feminine, and neuter.

One difference between Chaucerian English and present-day English which does not appear from the above diagram is a number distinction which cuts across that seen in sg. *I*, *ich*: pl. *we*; sg. *thou*, *thow*: pl. *ye*, etc. In the first and second genitives of the first and second persons we find the forms *my*, *myn*, *myne*; *thy*, *thyn*, *thyne*. These are all *singular* in the sense that they refer to a single person, *I* or *thou* respectively. But at the same time, in constructions like

> *my lord, myn ye,*
> *thy servant, thyn hors*, etc.,

the forms *my*, *myn*, *thy*, *thyn* are singular also in the sense that they are used to modify singular nouns, i.e. nouns referring to a single 'lord', 'eye', 'servant', 'horse', etc.

However, *myne*, and *thyne* in constructions like

> *myne eyen,*
> *thyne armes,*

while remaining singular in the sense that they refer to a single person, are also *plural*—and marked as such with the inflectional suffix *-e*, also used with plural adjectives—since they are used to modify plural nouns, i.e. nouns referring to more than one 'eye' and 'arm', etc.

A similar distinction is made also in the second genitive, cf.

> Thanne oughte she be *myn* PF 437,

as opposed to

> Thise been the cokkes wordes, and nat *myne* NPT 3265.

There are severe restrictions on the use of the *first* genitive plural forms *myne* and *thyne*. They occur only before words beginning with a vowel, and—since final *-e* is usually elided before a word beginning with a vowel—they are limited to the graphemic level.

Most of the other differences between the Chaucerian system and that found in present-day English will appear from the table on p. 57.

Among the more conspicuous differences are

(i)   the existence of second genitives identical in form with the corresponding first genitive:

hire, besides (more common) *hires* in the 3rd p.sg.fem.:

For this was his desir and *hire* also	MillT 3407,
I wol ben *hires*	PF 588;

oure, besides (more common) *oures* in the 1st p.pl.:

Oure is the voys	PF 545,
al this gold is *oures*	PardT 786;

youre, besides (more common) *youres* in the 2nd p.pl.:

Whan ye ben his al hool, as he is *youre*	Tr 2.587,
Hoom to myn hous, or elles unto *youres*	PardT 785.

(ii)   the use of *his* for the genitive in the 3rd p.sg. neuter:

That every sterre shulde come into *his* place Ther it was first . . .	PF 68,
In hire was everi vertu at *his* reste	PF 376;

the form *its* does not exist in Chaucerian English.

(iii)   the use of *hem* for the accusative in the 3rd p.pl. and *hir(e)*, *here* for the corresponding genitive:

So priketh *hem* nature in *hir* corages	Gen Prol 11.

Forms with initial *th-* are used occasionally by Chaucer to characterise the speech of Northerners, e.g. in the *Reeve's Tale*:

thair bodyes	RvT 4172.

About the other forms the following points should be noted:

1. The form *ich* /ɪtʃ/ in the 1st p.sg. is relatively rare. It occurs e.g. in MillT 3277. It is difficult to generalise about the relative frequency of such spelling variants as *thou:thow*; *hire:hir:hyre*; *thee:the*, etc. because different MSS tend to differ in their preferences. Thus while *thow* is very much a minority spelling in the CT, it is the only spelling used in the PF, which—it will be remembered—has a different textual history.

2. Something has been said already about the genitive forms of the first and second persons sg. It remains to be pointed out that the distribution of the *first* genitive forms with and without *-n* is phonologically conditioned, *my* and *thy* occurring before words beginning with a consonant other than /h/:[7]

> *my fader soule*,
> *my tale*;

while *myn* and *thyn* occur before words beginning with a vowel or with /h/:[7]

> *myn accord*,
> *thyn owene heed*,
> *myn herte*,
> *thyn hors*.

---

7. Assuming that initial *h* was pronounced in the words in question.

In addition it should be noted that when the genitive of the first person singular is used adjectivally in post-position in vocative constructions like

lemman myn	MillT 3700,
Cosyn myn	KnT 1081,
brother myn	MerchT 1521,

it takes the form *myn*.

3. Unusual or even abnormal forms are occasionally found in rhymes. Thus, to mention a few examples, in the *Clerk's Tale*, 508 we find the second person plural form *yee* in a syntactic function which requires the accusative:

> Ne I desire no thyng for to have,
> Ne drede for to leese, save oonly *yee*,

(rhyming with *me*, line 506). Some MSS have the singular form *thee*, which meets the syntactic requirement, but which is stylistically inappropriate: throughout the speech in which line 508 occurs Griselda uses the (appropriate) second person plural pronouns.
Conversely, in the same tale, line 106 *yow* occurs in the function of subject:

> For certes, lord, so wel us liketh *yow*
> And al youre werk, . . . that we
> Ne koude nat us self devysen how
> We myghte lyven in moore felicitee.

(The syntactic constructions into which the verb *liken* (LIKE) enters in Chaucerian English are such that there can be no doubt that *us* is the indirect object of *liketh* here and the subject of the verb is *yow And al youre werk*.)

A third unusual form occurring in rhyme is the accusative form *here* in the 3rd p.sg.fem. This form occurs occasionally in rhyme (generally with /æ:/-words); thus KnT, 1421, 2057, ClT 887, Tr 3.267, 4.612. Not only is the spelling *here* unusual for the accusative form of SHE in (the best MSS of) Chaucerian texts,[8] the vowel /æ:/ would also be an unusual vowel for this form, and if—as is commonly assumed—a final *-e* was pronounced in rhymes, we would have to assume that *here* was disyllabic in these rhymes. But metrical evidence strongly suggests that the normal forms *hire* and *hyre* were monosyllabic in Chaucerian texts.[9] But, of course, the *here*-rhymes may not have been perfect.

4. When the nominative form of the 2nd p.sg. is preceded by the verb in interrogative sentences, it often occurs in the form *-ou/ow*:

knowestow	(= 'knowest thou')	MillT 3156,
shaltou	(= 'shalt thou')	MillT 3575
woldestow	(= 'woldest thou')	NPT 3346

---

8. The form *here* is, however, found in the *genitive* feminine singular and in the third person genitive plural.
9. The first genitive forms *oure* and *youre* also seem to have been invariably monosyllabic.

The phenomenon can be explained as a merger of the preceding verb and the following pronoun. That such a merger does not always take place can be seen from PF 163:

Yit that thow canst not do, yit mayst thow se.

Interrogative/Relative Pronouns

WHO

The pronoun *who* reveals an inflection which is closely similar to that of personal pronouns:

Nominative	Accusative	Genitive (No morphological distinction between first and second.)	
who	whom	whos:	
who artow			MillT 3766,
I noot to *whom* it myght displese			NPT 3260,
if a preest be foul, on *whom* we truste			Gen Prol 501,
that fol (FOOL) of *whos* folie men ryme			Tr 1.532,
The formel on youre hond . . .			
Whos I am al			PF 419.

We are not here particularly concerned with the syntax of the forms under discussion, but it might be noted that while both *whom* and *whos* are freely used both as interrogative and as relative pronouns, there is no clear example of the nominative *who* as a relative in Chaucerian English. The compound *whoso*, however, frequently occurs as a so-called 'generalising relative', i.e. in the sense 'anyone who, whoever':

whoso list it nat yheere . . .
('Anyone who doesn't want to hear it . . .')   MillT 3176,
And *whoso* hit doth   PF 517.

Similarly *who that*; see e.g. PF 487.

WHICH

While *who* resembles personal pronouns in its inflection, *which* resembles adjectives in that it takes an -*e* in the plural:

a brooch . . . On *which* ther was   Gen Prol 161,
this Reve of *which* I telle . . .   Gen Prol 619,
He *which* that hath . . .   Gen Prol 836;

but

whiche they weren   Gen Prol 40,
herbes . . . The *whiche* han   NPT 2952,
paramours . . . Of *whiche* the faireste . . . Was   NPT 2869,

61

bemes . . . in *whiche* they blewe   NPT 3399,
hennes . . . *Whiche* were   NPT 2867,
etc.

In many cases the final /ə/ seems to have been dropped, but there is metrical evidence to suggest that sometimes at least it was pronounced. Consider e.g. the lines

Women inowe, of *whiche* some ther weere   PF 233,
Of *whiche* two Arcita highte that oon   KnT 1013,
Lo, *whiche* sleightes and subtilitees   MerchT 2421.

Similarly, a final *-e* is sometimes written and was apparently sometimes pronounced when *which(e)* was preceded by *the*:

The *whiche* vice he hydde, as he best myghte   WBT 955,
The *whiche* thynges troublen al this erthe   WBT 363,
Toward the *whiche* daunce he drow ful yerne   WBT 993,
Among the *whiche* pointz yspoken was   KnT 2972.

Though in this case we also find forms without *-e*:

                        . . . a parissh clerk,
The *which* that was ycleped Absolon   MillT 3313,
The *which* a long thyng were to devyse   ClT 52,
Save o thyng priketh in my conscience,
The *which* I wol reherce in youre presence   MerchT 1636.

Demonstrative Pronouns

There are two demonstrative pronouns in Chaucerian English which call for comment, viz. the two that are inflected for NUMBER (singular and plural):

Singular:	Plural:	
that	*tho*	Gen Prol 498, MillT 3246;
this	*thise*	Gen Prol 701, MillT 3564, etc.
	these	PF 141, 293, 432, etc.

The forms *thise* and *these* seem always to have been monosyllabic. And indeed the spellings *thes* and even *this* are found as plurals in some MSS.

Reflexive Pronouns

Pronouns in *-self* compounded with the accusative or first genitive form of the personal pronouns appear in the forms

-self,	e.g. *myself, thyself, hymself, hirself, itself, us self* (ClT 108), *your(e)self, hemself*;
-selve,	e.g. *myselve, thyselve, hymselve, hirselve, us selve* (ParsT 345–50), *your(e)selve, hemselve*;
-selven,	e.g. *myselven, thyselven, hymselven, hirselven, us selven* (WBT 812), *your(e)selven, hemselven*.

Note that *himselve* is sometimes used in the neuter:

ech thyng that is oned in *himselve*	SumT 1968.

Historically the forms in *-selve, -selven*, are inflected forms, but there is hardly any justification for regarding them as such in Chaucerian English. *-self-* and *-selve(n)*-forms seem to be used interchangeably in Chaucerian texts. Cf. e.g.

Wel oghte a wyf rather *hirselven* slee his wyf so deere	FranklT 1397,
Hirselven slow	FranklT 1415,

but

Hasdrubales wyf,	
That at Cartage birafte *hirself* hir lyf	FranklT 1400,
Hath nat Lucresse yslayn *hirself*, allas!	FranklT 1405.

It will be seen that in all these cases the syntax requires an 'accusative' or 'object' form of the reflexive pronoun. In other words no case distinction is expressed by the *-self*: *-selve(n)* opposition. Similarly, both *-f* and *-ve(n)*-forms are found in 'subject' position:

For he hadde power of confessioun,	
As seyde *hymself*, moore than a curat	Gen Prol 219,
he folwed it *hymselve*	Gen Prol 528,
I wol *myselven* goodly with yow ryde	Gen Prol 803.

Forms in *-selves* are not found in Chaucerian texts.

VERBS

Verbs in Chaucerian English are inflected for the following grammatical categories: TENSE (present and past), NUMBER (singular and plural), PERSON (only in the singular number, where a distinction is made between the first, second and third persons), and MOOD (indicative, subjunctive, and imperative). In addition three NON-FINITES have their distinct inflectional characteristics.

63

The Non-Finites

The non-finites are

1. The *infinitive*, formed by a voiced, alveolar, nasal suffix, spelt *-(e)n*, which has two allomorphs,

   /ən/,   used with the majority of verbs, e.g. *abyden, loven*; and

   /n/,   used with a limited number of verbs, whose bases end in a vowel,
   e.g. *don, fleen, gon, seyn, (seye(n)* is also found).

The *-n* suffix of the infinitive is very often dropped, and the *-e*, which becomes final through loss of /n/ is treated like other final /ə/'s in Chaucerian English, i.e. it is dropped or retained as required by the metre. (Cf. above, p. 16.) Thus the metre seems to require disyllabic forms of the infinitives in e.g.

To *ride* by the weye doumb as a stoon	Gen Prol 774,
To *telle* yow hir wordes and hir cheere	Gen Prol 728,
And for to *make* yow the moore mury	Gen Prol 802.

Whereas for instance in the following lines the infinitives seem to have been monosyllabic:

He was an esy man to *yeve* penaunce	Gen Prol 223,
Strong was the wyn, and wel to *drynke* us leste	Gen Prol 750,
To *kepe* his foreward by his free assent	Gen Prol 852.

2. The *present participle*, formed by the suffix /ɪng/, usually spelt *-ynge* or *-yng*, e.g.

Syngynge he was, or *floytynge*, al the day	Gen Prol 91,
a *whistlynge* wynd	Gen Prol 170,
A daggere *hangynge* on a laas	Gen Prol 392,
This Nicholas sat evere *capyng* upright	MillT 3444,
abidyng Goddes grace	MillT 3595,
. . . Was whilom *dewllyng* in a narwe cotage	NPT 2822.

3. The *past participle*. The formation of the past part. will be dealt with in detail later (pp. 65 ff.). Here it will be sufficient to point out

   (a) that the past part. often takes the prefix /ɪ/, spelt *y-* (or less frequently) *i-*, e.g.

   ybore Gen Prol 378, *ycome* Gen Prol 77,
   ycleped Gen Prol 376, *ydrawe* Gen Prol 396,
   ypreved Gen Prol 485, *ypunysshed* Gen Prol 657;
   ibounden PF 268, *ibroke* PF 282,
   ifounded PF 231, *imaked* PF 677;

   (b) that the past part. of those verbs which form the past tense and the past participle by means of a vowel replacive (cf. below pp. 71 ff.), often takes the suffix /ən/ or /n/, spelt -(e)n:

broken, songen, wonnen.

But, like the -(e)n of the infinitive, this suffix is frequently dropped. Consequently, a great many verbs have double forms in the past part.:

dryven:dryve; writen:write;
bigonnen:bigonne; wonnen:wonne;
broken:broke; born:bore;
fallen:falle, etc.

(c) that the past part. of those verbs which form the past tense and the past participle by means of the suffix /əd/ (cf. below), occasionally takes an additional suffix /ə/, but normally such participles remain uninflected:

the diverse causes of nature that weren
 yhidde (Bo I.m. 2.27),
Alle other dredes weren from him *fledde*
 (Tr 1.463).

We shall now consider in some detail the inflection of finite verbal forms in Chaucerian English.

Inflection for Tense

Traditionally verbs have been classified into two main classes, 'strong' (or 'vocalic') and 'weak' (or 'consonantal') (plus a few minor classes) according as the past tense and the past participle are formed by means of a vowel change (or 'vowel replacive'), as in

write — wrote — written

or by means of an inflectional suffix, as in

love — loved — loved.

Since this classification works less well for present-day English, and since one of our main concerns is a comparison between Chaucerian English and present-day English, the traditional classification will not be used here. The first basic distinction will be that between 'regular' and 'irregular' verbs.

REGULAR TENSE FORMATION

The *past tense* of verbs in Chaucerian English is regularly formed by adding the suffix /əd/, spelt -ed to the base of the verb, i.e. the verb stripped of its infinitive suffix /ən/ or /n/. The *past participle* is regularly formed in the same way:

arryve[10]	arryved	arryved,
assaye	assayed	assayed,
deme	demed	demed,
save	saved	saved.

That the *-ed* constituted a separate syllable in cases like *added*, *hated*, in which the base ends in an alveolar plosive, is beyond doubt. But there is substantial metrical evidence for the 'full' pronunciation /əd/ of the past tense and the past part. suffixes also in verbs in which the two suffixes do not constitute a separate syllable today. Consider for instance the following lines:

And *bathed* every veyne in swich licour	Gen Prol 3,
Hir over-lippe *wyped* she so clene . . .	Gen Prol 133,
But wel I woot he *lyed* right in dede	Gen Prol 659;
And they were *clothed* alle in o lyveree	Gen Prol 363,
. . . Why that *assembled* was this compaignye	Gen Prol 717,
. . . That was *arrayed* in that same wise	NPT 3037.

On the other hand, there is a certain amount of metrical evidence to suggest that the /ə/ of the regular past tense suffix and (somewhat more frequently) that of the past part. suffix was sometimes syncopated. (This means, of course, that the 'regularity' of the formation is here restricted to the graphemic level.)

Consider for instance

Wel *loved* he by the morwe a sop in wyn	Gen Prol 334,
For verray shame, and *blamed* hymself for he	
Had toold to me so greet a pryvetee	WBT 541,
And forth he *cleped* (/klept/?) a squier	
and a mayde	FranklT 1487;
This worthy lymytour was *cleped* (/klept/?) Huberd	Gen Prol 269,
For in his purs he sholde *ypunysshed* (/ɪˈpɔnɪʃt/?) be	Gen Prol 657,
And *batailled* as it were a castel wal	NPT 2860.

Sometimes the past tense suffix is spelt *-ede*. Metrical evidence suggests that the final *-e* of *-ede* was not normally pronounced:

So hoote he *lovede* that by nyghtertale	
He sleep namoore than . . .	Gen Prol 97,
Therefore he *lovede* gold in special	Gen Prol 444,
And *warnede* hym beforn of al his grace	PF 45.

But there is also metrical evidence to suggest that *-ede* was sometimes disyllabic:

10. In the lists of verbs given in this chapter those affixes that are not strictly part of the *tense* formation system have generally been disregarded, e.g. the *-(e)n* often found in the past plural, the *-(e)n* suffix of the infinitive, the *y*-prefix of the past participle, and normally also the *-(e)n* suffix of the past participle, if forms with and without *-(e)n* have been recorded. It should also be noted that usually no account is taken of such graphemic variation as that seen in e.g. *begynne:bygynne: bigynne; caughte:kaughte, wroot:wrot* (= 'wrote'), etc.

And of manhod hym *lakkede* right naught   Gen Prol 756,
Who *peyntede* the leon, tel me who?   WBT 692,
As I his suster *servede* by nyghte   ClT 640.

IRREGULAR TENSE FORMATION

By calling /əd/, -*ed*, the 'regular' allomorph of the past tense and past part. morphemes we have, of course, indirectly labelled all other allomorphs 'irregular'. We shall now consider the most important of these. It should be emphasised that neither the survey of irregular allomorphs that follows below nor the list of verbs given in any one sub-group is intended to be exhaustive. Also, even though, in cases where variant forms exist side by side, a relatively large number of variants have been listed, no attempt has been made to provide exhaustive lists of such variants. The irregular allomorphs fall into two or three main groups, which could be labelled (1) *additives*, in which a suffix is added to the base, (2) *replacives*, in which a vowel of the base is replaced by another vowel, and (3) *zero* allomorphs, in which there is no morphological distinction between present, past, and past part. (Quite often an additive occurs in combination with a replacive.)[11]

Additives

    1. Past tense -*de*, past part. -*d*
Some verbs form the past tense by adding /də/, spelt -*de*, to the base, and the past part. by adding /d/, spelt -*d*.

    Examples:

here	herde	herd,
leye	leyde	leyd,
pleye	pleyde	pleyd,
seye	seyde	seyd.

In a number of verbs the -*de*, -*d* suffixes are added to a base which has undergone some change compared with that found in the present system.[12] Thus in some verbs the additive is combined with a vowel replacive:

    (a) Replacive /e/ → /ɔː/:

selle	solde	soold,
telle	tolde	toold.

    (b) Replacive /iː/ → /ɪ/:

bityde	bitydde	bityd,
hyde	hydde	hyd.

    (c) Replacive /eː/ → /e/:

fede	fedde	fed,
spede	spedde	sped.

11. The terms 'additive', 'replacive', and 'zero' are used here to refer to *allomorphs of the past tense and past participle morphemes*. Instead of using the heavy and clumsy wording 'verbs whose past tense and past part. are formed by means of additive, replacive, or zero, allomorphs of the past tense and the past part. morphemes' we shall sometimes, for the sake of convenience, refer to these as 'additive', 'replacive', and 'zero' verbs, or simply—for the first two—'additives' and 'replacives'.
12. By the 'present system' is meant the infinitive, the forms of the present tense indicative and subjunctive, and the imperative.

The verbs in groups (b) and (c) are historically of the additive type (weak verbs). Thus in OE *hyde* and *feede* for instance appear as *hȳdan—hȳdde*, *fēdan—fēdde*. For Chaucerian English it might be argued that the past tense morpheme in these verbs takes the form of a vowel replacive:

/hi:də/   /hɪdə/   /hɪd/
/fe:də/   /fedə/   /fed/.

(True, there may have been a difference in consonant length between the present system and the past tense, the latter having a longer /d/ than the former, but consonant length was probably not phonemic in Chaucerian English.) There are, however, certain differences between the verbs in groups (b) and (c) on the one hand and replacives on the other. For one thing the past participle never takes the suffix /ən/ characteristic of replacives.[13] Secondly, the inflection for 2nd p.sg. past tense is of the type found with additives, i.e. with -*est* (*thou feddest, thou speddest*; cf. *thou songe, thou founde*).[14] For this reason the verbs are classified as additives in which the suffixes are added to a changed base. The base has in fact undergone a double change. Not only is the base vowel changed, but the final /d/ of the base is dropped before the suffixes are added.[15] Cf. a similar type of verb with -*te*, -*t* suffixes below, p. 71.

In connection with verbs of this type it should be borne in mind that elision of final /ə/ is liable to occur before vowels and /h/, if required by the metre. This means that besides past tense forms of the type /hɪdə/ there were alternative endingless forms like /hɪd/. An example is provided by WBT, line 745

Wher that hir housbonde hidde hym in a place,

in which the metre clearly suggests that *hidde* should be pronounced /hɪd/. Cf. also *had* besides *hadde* below.

(d) In some verbs the replacive /e:/ → /e/ alternates with /e:/ → /a/:

lede		ledde,		led,
	(more often)	ladde	(more often)	lad
rede		redde,		red,
		radde		rad
shede		shedde,		sched,
		shadde (in		shad
		rhyme MkT 2731)		
sprede		spradde		sprad,
				yspred (in rhyme
				RvT 4140).

A rather different change of base—loss of final consonant—is seen in

have   hadde   had.

---

13. The past participle *hidden* is a later formation.
14. On this see below, p. 85.
15. Alternatively one could say that the final /d/ of the base has merged with that of the suffix.

Alternative forms here are *han* in the infinitive (and present plural), and *had* in the past tense.

There is also a negative form *nadde* (= *ne hadde*); and in the 3rd p.sg. present indicative a form *nath* (= *ne hath*) occurs, e.g. WBT 100.

A verb which is historically of a very different type, but which in Chaucerian English has certain morphological affinities with the *-de, -d* verbs is

wol   wolde   wold.

The normal forms of this verb are

1st sg.	wol(e), wil[16] }	wolde	
2nd sg.	wolt, wilt[16] }	woldest	} wold.
3rd sg.	wol(e), wil[16] }	wolde	
Plural	wol(e)	wolde(n)	

There is also a corresponding negated verb

nyl   nolde.
nylt

2. Past tense *-te*, past part. *-t*

The *-te/-t* allomorphs are rare except in combination with replacives or other changes of the base. Examples of verbs with *-te/-t* added to unchanged base:

atteyne		atteynt
clappe	clapte	
spille		spilt.

Combined with changes of the base

(a) Replacive /eː/ → /e/:

lene ('lend')   lente   lent.

See also *fele, kepe*, etc., below, p. 78.

(b) In two verbs we find /eː/ → /e/ alternating with /eː/ → /a/ in the same way as under 1. (d) above. But in addition the *-te/-t*-verbs have a consonant replacive, the final /v/ of the base being replaced by the corresponding unvoiced fricative /f/:

leve	lefte, lafte	left, laft
reve ('rob')	refte, rafte	reft, raft.

16. Less frequent.

(c) A rather different type of replacive, also involving both vowels and consonants, is found in

quenche   queynte   queynt.[17]

(d) One verb drops a final /tʃ/ of the base:

fecche   fette   fet;

but the infinitive of this verb also occurs in the form *fette*, Tr 3.609 (in rhyme).

(e) Past tense /ɔʊxtə/, past part. /ɔʊxt/
A number of verbs whose present system is variously structured phonemically have in common a past tense in /ɔʊxtə/, spelt -*oughte* or -*oghte*, and a past part. in /ɔʊxt/, -*o(u)ght*:

(a)bye[18]	(a)boughte	(a)bo(u)ght
byseche,	bysoughte	
byseke		
bythynke,	bythoughte	bythoght
bythenke		
brynge	broughte	brought
recche ('care'),	roughte	
rekke		
seke,	soughte	sought
seche		
thynke,	thoughte	thought
thenke,		
thenche (in rhyme, MillT 3253)		
werke,	wroughte	wrought.
werche,		
wirche		

(f) A few have /aʊxtə/ in the past tense and /aʊxt/ in the past part.:

cacche	caughte	caught
reche ('reach')	raughte[19]	
teche	taughte	taught.

(g) Some verbs drop a final /d/ of the base before adding /tə/ and /t/:

bende	bente	bent
blende ('blind')	blente	blent
girde		girt
rende	rente	rent
sende	sente	sent
shende	shente	shent
wende	wente	went.

17. Cf. also *drenche*, below, p. 79.
18. *(a)beye* also occurs.
19. A past tense form *reighte* occurs in rhyme in HF 1374.

(h) In the three verbs

grete ('greet')	grette	gret
mete	mette	met
quite	quitte	quit

there is a replacive, long /e:/, /i:/ → short /e/, /ɪ/.
On the reason for treating these verbs as additives rather than as replacives see above p. 68.

Vowel Replacives

One notable difference between Chaucerian English and present-day English is found in the tense formation of those verbs which form the past tense (and the past part.) by means of a vowel replacive. A number of such verbs in Chaucerian English have a different vowel replacive in the past plural (and often also in the *second* person singular) from that found in the past singular (*first* and *third* persons). Thus the verb BEGIN in Chaucerian English normally takes the following forms:

Present system: *bigynn-*,
Past sg. 1st and 3rd persons: *bigan* (e.g. Gen Prol 44, KnT 1354),
Past sg. 2nd person: *bigonne* (e.g. Sec NT 442, Bo. 2.pr. 3.32),
Past plural: *bigonne* (e.g. FrT 1560, FranklT 1015),
Past part.: *bigonne*.

The term 'principal parts' is sometimes used for the four forms: the base of *the present system* (which, as has already been noted, comprises the infinitive, the forms of the present tense indicative and subjunctive, and the imperative), the *past singular* (comprising the 1st and 3rd persons past indicative), the *past plural* (comprising the base of the past plural indicative, the 2nd person past singular indicative, and the whole of the past subjunctive), and the *past participle*.
We shall now consider the most important of those verbs which form the past tense and the past part. by means of a vowel replacive. They will be sub-grouped on the basis of the type of replacive found in the principal parts. As will appear below, a number of verbs have variant forms in one or more of the principal parts (most often in the past sg., but also quite frequently in the past pl.). One of these is generally a new formation formed on analogy with one of the other principal parts of the verb in question. Thus the 3rd p.sg. past tense form *dronk*, which occurs in Tr 5.1440, is a historically 'incorrect' past sg. formed on analogy with the past plural and/or the past part., both of which had *dronk-*. Such 'new formations' are normally disregarded in the general characterisations of the groups of verbs given in the sub-headings below. These sub-headings, therefore, are to be regarded not as an attempt at a rigid classification, but rather as indicating certain 'basic patterns'. Another reason why a rigid sub-classification of verbs will not be attempted is that it is sometimes difficult to decide the exact nature of a given vowel replacive. Thus, for example, it seems obvious that in *syng-* → *sang* we have /ɪ/ replaced by a short /a/, and that in *syng* → *soong* /ɪ/ is replaced by a long vowel (/ɔ:/ or /o:/). But should *syng* → *song* be described as /ɪ/ replaced by short /o/ or as /ɪ/ replaced by a long vowel (/ɔ:/ or /o:/) with insufficient indication of vowel length?

1. Present system	Past sg.	Past pl.	Past part.
/iː/	/ɔː/	/ɪ/	/ɪ/
(a)byde	(a)bood		(a)byden
(a)ryse	(a)roos	arisen	(a)risen
glyde	glood		glyden
ryde	rood	riden	riden
smyte	smoot		smyten
write	wroot	writen	writen.

The two verbs

dryve	droof		dryven
stryve	stroof		stryven

have an additional /v/ → /f/ consonant replacive in the past singular. A similar replacive /z/ → /s/ in (a)ryse:(a)roos is not represented graphemically.

The difference in vowel quantity between the present system on the one hand and the past part. (and past pl.) on the other is obscured by the spelling. That there was a difference is revealed by the present-day English reflexes of the forms. As an example consider the behaviour of the verb DRIVE in rhyme. DRIVE appears as /draɪv/ in the present system today, but as /drɪvn/ in the past part. The infinitive (or present sg. subjunctive, which is formally identical with the endingless infinitive) in Chaucer rhymes with e.g. wyve KnT 1859, arryve MLT 469, on lyve Tr 5.665, stryve Tr 5.1551, all of which have present-day reflexes with /aɪ/, while the past part. rhymes with e.g. lyven (inf. of LIVE) and shryven (past part. of shryve) Tr 2.576, with lyven Tr 2.983, with yiven (inf. or past part. of GIVE) LGW 1924, 2430, all of which appear with short /ɪ/ today.

2. Present system	Past sg.	Past pl.	Past part.
/ɪ/	/a/	/ʊ/	/ʊ/
bygynne	bygan	bygonne	bygonne
drynke	drank[20]	dronke[20]	dronke
gynne	gan	gonne, gan[21]	
rynge	rong[22]	ronge	ronge
sprynge	sprang, sprong		spronge
spynne	span		sponne
synge	sang, so(o)ng	songe	songe
synke	sank		sonke
swymme		swommen	
swynke			swonke
wynne	wan		wonne.

20. As noted on p. 71 a 3rd p.sg. past tense form dronk occurs (Tr 5.1440). On the other hand, a 2nd p.sg. form drank is found at MkT 2226. Cf. pl. dronke in line 2228.
21. Gan is rare in the pl., but does occur, e.g. BD 1312, LGW 1501.
22. No sg. with a recorded.

3. Present system /i:/	Past sg. /o/ or /ɔː/[23]	Past pl. /u:/	Past part. /u:/
bynde	bo(o)nd,	bounde	bounde[24]
clymbe	clomb[25]	cloumbe, clombe, clambe	cloumbe, clombe
fynde	fo(o)nd,[26] found	founde,[26] fonde	founde
grynde	grond		grounde.

4. Present system /e/ or /æː/[27]	Past sg. /a/	Past pl. /o/ or /ʊ/	Past part. /o/
melte	malt		molte
renne	ran	ronne[28]	ronne
stele	stal		stole
swelle	swal		swollen
trede	trad	troden	troden
yelde	yald		yolden.

A few of the verbs of this group show an additional replacive /v/ → /f/ in the past sg. (Cf. *dryve—droof* and *stryve—stroof* above, p. 72.)

delve	dalf	dulve	dolven
kerve	karf	korve	korve
sterve	starf	storve	storve
weve	waf		woven.

The following verbs can all be said to follow the basic pattern of group 4, but with greater or smaller deviations:

(a)wreke	wrak		(a)wreke, (a)wroken
bere	ba(a)r, beer (in rhyme)	bare, beren (in rhyme)	bore
breke	brak	breeke	broke

23. Spellings like *boond*, *foond* clearly indicate a long vowel (/ɔː/). It is not easy or indeed possible to decide whether *bond*, *fond*, etc. had the same long vowel, 'insufficiently' marked for length in the spelling, or the short vowel /o/.
24. A past part. form *bonde* occasionally occurs in rhymes, e.g. MkT 2270, WBT 378, Tr 1.255, 2.1223.
25. Past sg. also *clamb* (Thop 797).
26. There is a very strong tendency for *fo(o)nd* forms to be used in the past sg. and *founde* in the past pl., but occasionally *found* occurs in the sg. (e.g. BD 1163, Tr 3.536), and *fonde* occurs at least once in the pl. (HF 1810).
27. The spelling and/or the later development of some of these verbs suggest(s) a long vowel /æː/ in the present system, e.g. *stele*, *yelde*, *weve*; others had the short /e/, e.g. *melte*, *swelle*.
28. A past pl. *ran* occurs in rhyme in NPT 3381, and another (line 3385) may be due to false concord between subject and verb.

breste	brast	broste, braste, bruste	broste
(for)bede, bidde	(for)bad	bede	(for)bode, bede
(for)swere	forswor, swo(o)r	swore	(for)swore
chese	chees	chose	chose
helpe	heelp (KnT 1651, MkT 2046, MLT 920)		holpe
heve ('heave')	ha(a)f, hef		
speke	spak	speke, spake	spoke.

5. A relatively large group of verbs have the same vowel (or diphthong) in the past part. as in the present system.
Several sub-groups are discernible:

bake			bake
(bi)take	(bi)took	tooke	(bi)take
forsake	forso(o)k		forsake
shake	shook		shake
shape	shoop	shope	shape
(bi)knowe	(bi)knew	(bi)knewe	(bi)knowe
crowe	crew		crowe
sowe ('sow')			sowe
throwe	threw		throwe
drawe	drew, drow, drough		drawe
forgete, foryete	forgat, foryat	forgate	forgeten, foryeten
gete	gat		gete
foryeve, foryive	foryaf,[29] forgaf	forgave	foryeve, foryive
yeve, yive	yaf[29]	yave[30]	yeve, yive
bete		beete, bette	bete
ete	eet	ete	ete
frete		freete	frete
lete[31]	leet	leete	lete[31]

29. With the /v/ → /f/ replacive also found elsewhere, cf. above pp. 72 and 73.
30. There seems to be a distinction between past sg. *yaf* and past pl. *yave(n)*, though *yaf* occurs at least once as a plural (Gen Prol 302). The 3rd sg. form *yave* which occurs in rhyme in Tr 2.977 is a subjunctive.
31. Also *late(n)*.

(bi)holde[32]	(bi)held	(bi)helde	(bi)holde
stonde	stood	stode	stonde
(bi)falle	(bi)fel(le), (bi)fil(le)	felle, (bi)fille	(bi)falle
wasshe	wessh	wesshe	wasshe
waxe,	wexe,	wexe,	waxe,
wexe	we(e)x, wax	woxe	woxe
come	cam, came, com, come	cam, come	come.

Two verbs which are historically rather different from the verbs in this group are DO and GO. They agree with group 5 verbs, however, in having the same vowel in the past part. as in the present system. The past tense forms are of an entirely different type (suffix -*de* added to changed base):

do(o)	dide	dide	do(o)n, do
go(o)	yede	yede	go(o)n, go.

The *yede* forms are very rare and occur only in rhyme, e.g. CYT 1141, 1281; Tr 5.843. The past tense of GO is regularly supplied by *wente* from *wende*. Cf. above p. 70.

6. The verbs listed below do not easily fit into any of the 'basic patterns' given above:

fighte	faught	fo(u)ghte	fougthen
lye, ligge	lay	laye	leyn
se	saugh, sawgh, saw, say, sy,[34] seigh, sigh[34]	sawe, syen, saughe, saye	seyn,[33] sene[33]
sitte	sat, sete, sate	sete, sat, sate	seten
slee	slow, slough	slowe	slawe, slayn.

32. An infinitive form *(be)helde* occurs in rhyme (WBT 272, Anel 80).
33. The normal past part. form is *seyn*; *sene* occurs mostly in rhyme.
34. E.g. *sy* CYT 1381, *sigh* HF 1162, 1429 (all three in rhyme).

A unique consonant replacive in the past part. is found in

sethe	seeth	sode.

Two verbs call for special comments:

bihote,	bihighte,	bihight,
bihete	bihette	

used in the sense of 'promise', is relatively straightforward.

The past sg. form *behette* occurs in rhyme (PF 436). But the corresponding verb without the prefix *bi-/be-* is rather complex. For one thing a number of variant forms occur:

hote,	highte,	hight,
he(e)te,[35]	hatte,	hoote.
highte	he(e)t	

Secondly, the verb is used in rather different senses: 'be called' (e.g. Gen Prol 616, KnT 1557); 'promise' (KnT 2398, ClT 496); 'command' (HF 1719). It is difficult to decide to what extent a semantic differentiation between the variant forms may have been attempted. But it may be noted that the *present* tense forms *highte* occur only in the sense 'be called', while the *hote*, *he(e)te* forms are used both in the sense 'be called' and in the sense 'promise'. In the past tense *highte*-forms are found both in the sense 'be called' and in the sense 'promise', but *hatte*, *heet*, *het* only occur in the sense 'be called'. The past participle form *hoote* (RvT 3941) is used in the same sense ('be called'), while the *hight*-forms are used in the sense 'promise'. Whether or not these semantic correlations reflect deliberate semantic differentiation, or are random and simply depend on the small number of occurrences in the Chaucer canon, is difficult to decide.

Zero Verbs

By zero verbs is meant verbs which have zero allomorphs of the past tense and past participle morphemes.[36] Among such verbs are

alighte	alighte	alight
(bi)sette	(bi)sette	(bi)set
dighte ('prepare')	dighte	dight
hente	hente	hent
hurte	hurte[37]	hurt
knytte		knyt
liste ('please')	liste	

35. The present tense forms *he(e)te* occur in rhyme, e.g. KnT 2398, MLT 334, BD 1226.
36. On p. 67 above 'zero allomorph' was used with reference to verbs in which there is no morphological distinction between present, past, and past part. It will now be seen that this statement, applied to the verbs in this group, actually represents an over-simplification. Since the past part. of the verbs in question does not normally take a suffix, there *is*, of course, a morphological distinction between the past part. on the one hand and the present and past tense on the other, in that the latter forms normally do take a suffix. However, as we have seen, *-(e)n* suffixes are often dropped.
37. A past tense form *herte* occurs in rhyme (with *herte* (HEART)) in BD 883.

plighte	plighte	plight
putte	putte	put
shette	shette	shet
sterte	sterte	stert
swelte ('die', 'faint')	swelte.	

It will be seen that the verbs in this group generally have bases ending in -t. (There are also a very few ending in -d, e.g. (a)breyde.)

The verb

lepe ('leap') leep,

of which no past part. has been recorded in Chaucerian texts, is historically a 'strong' verb, but is strictly speaking a 'zero verb' in Chaucerian English—provided, of course, that the present and the past had the same long 'e'-vowel.

The Verb to be

This verb is very irregular:

Infinitive:		be, been, ben
Present tense:	1st p.sg.ind.:	am
	2nd p.sg.ind.:	art
	3rd p.sg.ind.:	is
	sg. subjunctive:	be
	pl.ind. and subj.:	ben, been, be, *more rarely* ar, are, arn
Imperative:	sg.:	be
	pl.:	be, beth
Past tense:	1st p.sg.ind.:	was
	2nd p.sg.ind.:	were
	3rd p.sg.ind.:	was
	sg. subjunctive:	were
	pl. ind. and subj.:	were, weren
Past part.:		been, ben, be.

Some of these have negative counterparts:

nam (= *ne am*), nart (= *ne art*), nys, nis, nas (= *ne was*), nere (= *ne were*).

Verbs Vacillating between Different Classes

So far we have seen that some verbs have variant forms in one or more of their principal parts. But the variants considered so far have been relatively minor in the sense that they have not affected the classification of the verbs in question. Thus the past plural of e.g. *breste*, is *broste*, *braste*, and *bruste*, but in any case the tense formation is of a replacive type. Quite a number of Chaucerian verbs, however, have variant forms which cut across the basis of classification adopted in this book. Consequently, these verbs must be said to vacillate between different classes.

1. Verbs vacillating between the 'regular' and an 'irregular' class of verbs
   (a) Vacillation between -ed and -de/-d

answere	answered, answerde	answered, answerd
crie	cried, cride	cried, cryd
deye, dye	deyed, deyde, dyed, dyde	dyed, deyd
(ful)fille	fulfilled, fulfilde	(ful)filled, (ful)fild
paye	payde	payed, payd
preye	preyed, preyde	preyed.

In two verbs the -de/-d suffix is added to a changed base:

kithe ('make known')	kithed, kidde	kyd
make	maked, made	maked, maad.

(b) Vacillation between -ed and -te/-t

dwelle	dwelled, dwelte	dwelled, dwelt
kysse	kyssed, kiste	kist
passe	passed, paste[38]	passed, past[38]
presse	pressed	prest
spende	spente	spent, ispendid.

In the following verbs the -te/-t additive is combined with some replacive:

dele	deled, delte	. deled
fele	feled, felte	feled, felt
kepe	keped, kepte	kept
mene	mened, mente	ment
bireve	birefte, birafte	bireved, bireft, biraft

38. The past(e) forms occur in rhyme.

drenche	dreynte	drenched, dreynt
sike ('sigh')	siked, sighte	
strecche	straughte, streighte	strecched, straught, streyght.

(c) Vacillation between *-ed* and vowel replacive

(a)wake	(a)waked, (a)wo(o)k,	(a)waked, wakened
clawe	clawed, clew	clawed
growe	growed, grew	growe
honge, hange	hanged, he(e)ng	hanged
laughe	lough	laughed, laughen
quake	quo(o)k	quaked
shyne	shyned, sho(o)n, shynen (past pl.) (KnT 2043)	
walke	walked, welk	walked.

(d) Vacillation between *-ed* and zero

asterte	asterted, asterte	astert
cutte, kitte	kitte	cutted, cut
enoynte	enoynte	enoynted, enoynt
laste	lasted, laste	
stynte, stente[39]	stynte, stente[39]	stynted, stynt, stent.[39]

2. Verbs vacillating between two 'irregular' classes

(a) Vacillation between *-de/-d* and *-te/-t*

brenne, brynne	brende, brente	brend,[40] brent.

---

39. The *stent*(e) forms occur in rhyme.
40. A form *burned* occurs as an attributive adjectival in the phrase *burned gold*. Historically this belongs to a different verb (OF *burnir*).

79

(b) Vacillation between -de/-d and vowel replacive

In all three verbs in this group the -de/-d suffix is combined with a vowel replacive:

fare	ferde	ferd, faren	
flee (= 'flee')	fledde, fleigh	fled	
flee (= 'fly')	fleigh, fley	flowen, (thou) flaugh	flowen, fled.

The two verbs *flee* (= 'flee' and = 'fly') are mostly kept apart in Chaucerian English. But on at least two occasions they are mixed up. *Fleigh*, which is the normal past sg. of *flee* in the sense 'fly' occurs in the sense 'fled' in MkT 2689, and the additive participle *yfled* occurs once in the sense 'flown' in Tr 4.661.

(c) Vacillation between -te/-t and vowel replacive

Again the -te/-t suffix is combined with some replacive in all verbs in question (usually a vowel replacive, but in *cleve—clefte* the vowel replacive (/e:/? → /e/) is combined with /v/ → /f/, which we have seen before):

biwepe	biwepte	biwopen
cleve ('split')	clefte	cloven
crepe	crepte, cre(e)pe	crept, cropen
lese	loste, les	lost, lorn, lore
slepe	slepte, sleep	
wepe	wepte, we(e)p	wept, wopen, wepen.

(d) The past participle of the 'zero' type verb

caste	caste	cast

occurs once as *casten* (the *Prioress's Tale*, line 606), which is of the type characteristic of replacive verbs.

Preterite-Present Verbs

A small group of strongly irregular verbs are traditionally referred to as 'preterite-present verbs'. They are verbs whose present tense forms are historically 'preterites' or past tense forms. This fact is revealed by the formal resemblance which some of the present tense forms of the verbs in question in Chaucerian English bear to the *past* tense forms of certain replacive verbs. Thus the *present* tense form 1st and 3rd sg. *can*, plural *conne*, should be compared with *past* tense forms like 1st and 3rd sg. *gan/ran*, plural *gonne/ronne*. Once the old 'preterites' had acquired a present tense meaning (through a semantic shift which took place in prehistoric times) the need arose for a new past tense form, and new past tense forms (of the additive type) were then created. Cf. *coude*. Most of the verbs in question are of very high frequency. Most of them are also defective, i.e. one or more of the principal parts are lacking or extremely rare. The most important verbs in question are:

Infinitive:		conne
Present tense:	1st and 3rd sg.:	can
	2nd sg.	canst
	plural:	conne, can (e.g. MLT 622)
Past tense:		coude, couthe
Past part.:		coud, couth.

Infinitive:		durre
Present tense:	1st and 3rd sg.:	dar
	2nd sg.	darst
	plural	dar, dare
Past tense:		dorste, durste.

Present tense:	1st and 3rd sg.:	moot, mote, moste
	2nd sg.:	most
	plural:	moote, mooten, moste, mosten
Past tense:		moste.

The form *moste* is historically the new past tense form, created after the etymon of *moot* had acquired a present tense meaning (cf. above). It is clear, however, that *moste* in Chaucerian English is sometimes used in contexts which require a present tense interpretation of the form. See e.g. KnT 1290, 3088, MillT 3297, Tr 2.894. These should be contrasted with e.g. MerchT 1966, Tr 5.70 in which *moste* occurs in past tense contexts.

Infinitive:		mowe
Present tense:	1st and 3rd sg.:	may
	2nd sg.:	mayst
	plural:	mowe(n), may
Past tense:		myghte.

Present tense:	1st sg.:	owe, o(u)ghte
	2nd sg.:	owest, o(u)ghtest
	3rd sg.:	oweth, o(u)ghte
	plural:	owe, owen, o(u)ghte(n)
Past tense:		o(u)ghte
Past part.:		owed.

The history of this verb is rather complex and will not, of course, be considered in any detail here. But it might be noted that the primary sense of the verb in OE was 'possess', 'own'. That this sense is sometimes retained in Chaucerian English is revealed by constructions like

the good-man that the beestes oweth   PardT 361.

Fairly early the verb came to be used in the sense 'be under an obligation to (re)pay, give', etc. (present-day English *owe*). This sense is found several times in Chaucer, but is mostly restricted to the present tense forms, *owe, owest, oweth, owe(n)*; e.g.

we *owen* fourty pound	SumT 2106,
dette which thou *owest* me of old	FrT 1615,
I ne *owe* hem nat a word	WBT 425,
his love, the which that he *oweth* al to God	ParsT 365–70.

There is, however, at least one example of a past tense form *oughte* used in this sense in Chaucerian English, viz.

And, as Fortune hire *oughte* a foul myschaunce,	
She wex enamoured upon this man	LGW 1609.

On the other hand, a new 'regular' past part. of the verb used in this sense is found in the translation of *Boethius*:

prisown, lawe, and thise othere tormentz of laweful	
peynes ben rather *owed* to felonus citezeins	Bo 4.pr.5.16.

By far the commonest sense of the verb in Chaucerian English is that of '(moral) obligation', (= present-day English *ought*). There are relatively few examples of *owe-* forms used in this sense:

ye *owen* to enclyne and bowe youre herte	Mel 1500–05,
the fruites of the erthe *owen* to be to the	
noryssynge of beestis	Bo 2.pr.5.74,
we *owe* to graunte that . . .	Bo 3.pr.10.57,
And . . . hym *oweth*,[41] of verray duetee,	
Shewen his peple pleyn benygnete	LGW G 360.

The vast majority of occurrences of the verb in this sense take the form *o(u)ght(-)*. Historically, this is the 'new' past tense form, created after the prehistoric semantic shift discussed above (p. 81), but—like *moste* (cf. above)— *o(u)ghte* very often occurs in present tense contexts; e.g.

As monkes been—or elles *oghte* be—	PrT 643,
I wol yow telle a litel thyng in prose	
That *oghte* liken yow	Thop 938,

which should be compared with e.g. Tr 2.912, and Tr 3.581, in which *oughte* occurs in past tense contexts.

Present tense:	1st and 3rd sg.:	shal
	2nd sg.:	shalt
	plural:	shul, shulle, shal
Past tense:		sholde.

41. The verb is quite often used in 'impersonal constructions', as here.

Infinitive:			wite
Present tense:	1st and 3rd sg.:		wo(o)t
	2nd sg.:		wo(o)st
	plural:		wite(n), wo(o)t
Past tense:			wiste
Past part.:			wist.

The corresponding negated verb is

Present tense:	1st and 3rd sg.:	no(o)t
	2nd sg.:	nost
Past tense:		nyste.

Inflection for Number Person and Mood

The remaining types of verbal inflection are best treated together. There are certain minor differences between additives and replacives (especially in the past tense) which make it desirable to keep these apart in our discussion. We shall use the verbs LOVE and SAY to illustrate the inflection of additives and HOLD and SING as illustrations of the inflection of replacives. We shall then add such comments as seem to be called for. Since the inflections are not the same in the present system and in the past tense, these two will be treated separately.

The Present System

Infinitive			love(n)[42]	sey(n)
Indicative Mood	Singular	1st p.:	love	sey(e)
		2nd p.:	lovest[43]	sey(e)st
		3rd p.:	loveth[43]	seyth
	Plural:		love(n)	sey(n)
Subjunctive Mood	Singular:		love	sey(e)
	Plural:		love(n)	sey(n)
Imperative Mood	Singular:		love	sey
	Plural:		loveth	sey(e)th

42. Brackets indicate alternative forms.
43. Very occasionally 2nd and 3rd p.sg. forms in *-es* occur in rhyme; e.g. 2nd p. *brynges* rhyming with *tydynges*) in HF 1908; 3rd p. *telles* (rhyming with *elles* ('else') in BD 73; 3rd p. *falles* (rhyming with *halles*) in BD 257. The *-es* in the 2nd and 3rd p.sg. is a feature characteristic of Northern dialects in ME times.

			holde(n)	synge(n)
Infinitive			holde(n)	synge(n)
Indicative Mood	Singular	1st p.:	holde	synge
		2nd p.:	holdest	syngest
		3rd p.:	holdeth, halt	syngeth
	Plural:		holde(n)	synge(n)
Subjunctive Mood	Singular:		holde	synge
	Plural:		holde(n)	synge(n)
Imperative Mood	Singular:		hold	syng
	Plural:		holdeth	syngeth.

As will be seen, the differences between the two types of verb in the present system are negligible.

The -est and -eth suffixes in the second and third persons sg. indicative sometimes, but not always, constitute separate syllables. In some verbs this may be indicated by the spelling, as when *seyest* occurs side by side with *seyst*. In other cases there is metrical evidence to suggest that the vowel was sometimes syncopated. Compare e.g.

Who *loveth* best this gentil formel heere   PF 535,
She *loveth* so this hende Nicholas   MillT 3386

with

Al that now *loveth* asondre sholde lepe   Tr 3.1763,
That *loveth* hire housbonde as hire hertes lyf   FranklT 816.

Cf. also the following line from the *Wife of Bath's Tale*,

And *taketh* his leve, and *wendeth* forth his weye (918),

which can be made to scan by syncopating the vowel /ə/ in *taketh*, but not in *wendeth*.

In quite a few replacive verbs syncopation of /ə/ in the third person sg. has had more far-reaching repercussions on the phonemic structure of the form. A number of verbs, therefore, have doublets in the 3rd p.sg. present indicative, a 'full' form existing side by side with a syncopated one in which further phonological changes have occurred. Thus we find *rideth* (e.g. KnT 1691) besides *rit* (e.g. KnT 974, 981). Quite often such 'further phonological changes' have affected the vowel of the base. Thus a long vowel is shortened in *bynt* (besides *byndeth*, which probably had the same long vowel as that of the infinitive) and *fynt* (besides *fyndeth*). A change of vowel is also seen in *halt* besides *holdeth* (cf. the paradigm given above), and in this case there is also a change of vowel quality not just vowel quantity. Similarly, we find *stant* besides *stondeth*. This phenomenon is found particularly with verbs whose bases end in an alveolar plosive, but is not limited to such verbs; cf. *arist* (MLT 265) besides *aryseth*, *rist* (MillT 3688) besides *ryseth*, *drifth* (Tr 5.1332) (with consonant change /v/ → /f/) besides *dryveth*, etc.

The -*(e)n* of the present plural, indicative and subjunctive, is often dropped, in the same way as that of the infinitive.

The imperative plural sometimes drops the -*th* suffix. Compare e.g.

	Holdeth youre heste	FranklT 1064
with		
	Hoold up youre hondes	Gen Prol 783.
Similarly,		
	Telleth youre tale	FrT 1289,
	Now *telleth* forth	FrT 1336

should be compared with

Tel forth youre tale	FrT 1300,
Tel me anon	Gen Prol 808,
Telle us a tale anon	MLT 34.

The Past Tense System

	1st p.sg.:	loved	seyde
Singular	2nd p.sg.:	lovedest	seydest
	3rd p.sg.:	loved	seyde
Plural:		loved, lovede(n)	seyd, seyde(n)
	1st p.sg.:	heeld	sang, so(o)ng
Singular	2nd p.sg.:[44]		songe
	3rd p.sg.:	heeld	sang, so(o)ng
Plural:		helde(n)	songe(n).

We have seen before (p. 71) that in replacive verbs there is sometimes a difference between the vowel of the 1st and 3rd persons sg. on the one hand and that of the plural and the 2nd person sg. on the other. This distinction is not made by all replacive verbs, e.g. not by *holde*.

The distinction between the indicative and the subjunctive is not kept up in the past tense to the same extent as in the present. For this reason it has been disregarded in the past tense paradigm given above.

---

44. No 2nd p.sg. form of this verb has been recorded in Chaucerian texts. There is little reason to doubt that it would have appeared in some such form as *helde*, had it been recorded.

Appendix

Alphabetical list of irregular verbs

The list given below contains only those verbs which have been dealt with in this book. This means that the list is not intended to be exhaustive. (Cf. what was said about the discussion of irregular tense formation above, p. 67.) Nor have all variants been included in all cases where alternative forms exist side by side. For these details the reader is referred to the discussion of irregular tense formation, pp. 67–80. (But again it should be noted that the discussion found there is not intended to be exhaustive in the sense that it includes all variants found in Chaucerian English.)

The verbs in the list appear in strict alphabetical order (except that variant infinitive forms have not always been given alphabetically). Readers should therefore bear in mind what has been said about spelling variation in Chaucerian texts. Thus the prefix BE- usually appears as *bi-* and *by-*, and the verbs in question are listed accordingly, *bifalle* (= BEFALL), for instance, occurring after *bidde*, and *bygynne* (= BEGIN) after *bye* (= BUY). Similarly, *synge* (= SING), of which no *i*-spelling occurs, should be sought after *sw-*, etc.

INFINITIVE	PAST SG.	PAST PL.	PAST PART.
abyde ('stay')	abood		abyden
abye ('pay for')	aboughte		abo(u)ght
alighte	alighte		alight
answere	answered, answerde		answered, answerd
aryse	aros	arisen	arisen
asterte ('escape')	asterted, asterte		astert
atteyne			atteynt
awake	awaked, awo(o)k		awaked

86

INFINITIVE	PAST SG.	PAST PL.	PAST PART.
awreke ('avenge')			awreke, awroken
bake			bake
be	was	were	been, ben, be
bede see *bidde*			
bende	bente		bent
bere ('carry')	ba(a)r, beer	bare, beren	bore
bete ('beat')		beete, bette	bete
bidde, bede	bad	bede	bode, bede
bifalle ('happen')	bifel, bifil	bifille	bifalle
bihete see *bihote*			
biholde, bihelde	biheld	bihelde	biholde
bihote, ('promise') bihete	bihighte, bihette		bihight
biknowe ('acknowledge')	biknew	biknewe	biknowe
bireve ('deprive of')	birefte, birafte		bireved, bireft, biraft
bisette ('bestow')	bisette		biset
bitake ('entrust')	bitook		bitake
bityde ('happen')	bitydde		bityd
biwepe ('lament')	biwepte		biwopen
blende ('blind')	blente		blent
breke ('break')	brak	breeke	broke
brenne, ('burn') brynne	brende, brente		brend, brent
breste ('burst')	brast	broste, braste, bruste	broste
brynge	broughte		brought
brynne see *brenne*			
byde ('wait')	bood		byden
bye ('buy')	boughte		bo(u)ght
bygynne	bygan	bygonne	bygonne
bynde	bo(o)nd	bounde	bounde
byseche, byseke	bysoughte		
bythynke, bythenke	bythoughte		bythoght
cacche ('catch')	caughte		caught
caste ('throw')	caste		cast, casten

INFINITIVE	PAST SG.	PAST PL.	PAST PART.
chese ('choose')	chees	chose	chose
clappe	clapte		
clawe ('scratch')	clawed, clew		clawed
cleve ('split')	clefte		cloven
clymbe	clomb, clamb	cloumbe, clombe, clambe	cloumbe, clombe
come	cam, came, com, come	cam, come	come
crepe	crepte, cre(e)pe		crept, cropen
crie	cried, cride		cried, cryd
crowe	crew		crowe
cutte, kitte	kitte		cutted, cut
dele ('deal')	deled, delte		deled
delve	dalf	dulve	dolven
deye, ('die') dye	deyed, deyde, dyed, dyde		dyed, deyd
dighte ('prepare')	dighte		dight
do	dide	dide	do(o)n, do
drawe	drew, drow, drough		drawe
drenche ('drown')	dreynte		drenched, dreynt
drynke	drank, dronk	dronke, drank	dronke
dryve	droof		dryven
dwelle	dwelled, dwelte		dwelled, dwelt
enoynte	enoynte		enoynted, enoynt
ete	eet	ete	ete
falle	fille, fil, felle, fel	fille, felle	falle
fare ('go')	ferde		ferd, faren

INFINITIVE	PAST SG.	PAST PL.	PAST PART.
fecche, ('fetch')	fette		fet
fette			
fede	fedde		fed
fele	feled,		feled,
	felte		felt
fette see *fecche*			
fighte	faught	fo(u)ghte	foughten
fille (see also *fulfille*)			filled,
			fild
flee ('flee')	fledde,		fled
	fleigh		
flee ('fly')	fleigh,	flaugh,	flowen,
	fley	flowen	fled
forbede	forbad		forbode
forgete,	forgat,	forgate	forgeten,
foryete	foryat		foryeten
forsake	forso(o)k		forsake
forswere	forswor		forswore
foryete see *forgete*			
foryeve,	foryaf,	forgave	foryeve,
foryive	forgaf		foryive
frete ('devour')		freete	frete
fulfille	fulfilled,		fulfilled,
	fulfilde		fulfild
fynde	fo(o)nd,	founde,	founde
	found	fonde	
gete	gat		gete
girde			girt
glyde	glood		glyden
go	yede	yede	go(o)n,
			go
grete	grette		gret
growe	growed,		growe
	grew		
grynde	grond		grounde
gynne ('begin')	gan	gonne,	
		gan	
hange,	hanged,		hanged
honge	he(e)ng		
have	hadde		had
here	herde		herd
heete see *hote*			
helpe	heelp		holpe
hente ('seize')	hente		hent
hete see *hote*			
heve ('heave')	ha(a)f,		
	hef		
highte see *hote*			
holde,	held	helde	holde
helde			

INFINITIVE	PAST SG.	PAST PL.	PAST PART.
honge see *hange*			
hote, ('be called')	highte,		hight,
he(e)te,	hatte,		hoote
highte	he(e)t		
hurte	hurte		hurt
hyde	hydde		hyd
kepe	kepte,		kept
	keped		
kerve ('carve')	karf	korve	korve
kithe ('make known')	kithed,		kyd
	kidde		
kitte see *cutte*			
knowe	knew	knewe	knowe
knytte			knyt
kysse	kyssed,		kist
	kiste		
laste	lasted,		
	laste		
laughe	lough		laughed,
			laughen
lede ('lead')	ledde,		led,
	ladde		lad
lene ('lend')	lente		lent
lepe ('leap')	leep		
lese ('lose')	loste,		lost,
	les		lorn,
			lore
lete ('let')	leet	leete	lete
leve ('leave')	lefte,		left,
	lafte		laft
leye ('lay')	leyde		leyd
ligge see *lye*			
liste ('please')	liste		
lye,	lay	laye	leyn
ligge			
make	maked,		maked,
	made		maad
melte	malt		molte
mene ('mean')	mened,		ment
	mente		
mete	mette		met
passe	passed,		passed,
	paste		past
paye	payde		payed,
			payd
pleye	pleyde		pleyd
plighte ('pledge')	plighte		plight
presse	pressed		prest

INFINITIVE	PAST SG.	PAST PL.	PAST PART.
preye	preyed, preyde		preyed
putte	putte		put
quake	quo(o)k		quaked
quenche	queynte		queynt
quite ('reward')	quitte		quit
recche, ('care') rekke	roughte		
reche ('reach')	raughte, reighte		
rede ('read')	redde, radde		red, rad
rekke see *recche*			
rende	rente		rent
renne ('run')	ran	ronne, ran	ronne
reve ('rob')	refte, rafte		reft, raft
ryde	rood	riden	riden
rynge	rong	ronge	ronge
ryse	roos		risen
se	saugh, sawgh, saw, say, sy, seigh, sigh	sawe, syen, saughe saye	seyn, sene
seke, seche	soughte		sought
selle	solde		soold
sende	sente		sent
sethe ('boil')	seeth		sode
sette	sette		set
seye	seyde		seyd
shake	shook		shake
shape	shoop	shope	shape
shede ('shed')	shedde, shadde		sched, shad
shende ('ruin')	shente		shent
shette ('shut')	shette		shet
shyne	shyned, sho(o)n	shynen	
sike ('sigh')	siked, sighte		
sitte	sat, sete, sate	sete, sat, sate	seten

INFINITIVE	PAST SG.	PAST PL.	PAST PART.
slee ('slay')	slow, slough	slowe	slawe, slayn
slepe	slepte, sleep		
smyte	smoot		smyten
sowe ('sow')			sowe
spede ('succeed')	spedde		sped
speke	spak	speke, spake	spoke
spende	spente		spent, ispendid
spille ('destroy')			spilt
sprede	spradde		sprad, spred
sprynge	sprang, sprong		spronge
spynne	span		sponne
stand see *stonde*			
stele	stal		stole
stente see *stynte*			
sterte ('leap')	sterte		stert
sterve ('die')	starf	storve	storve
stonde	stood	stode	stonde
strecche	straughte, streighte		strecched, straught, streyght
stryve	stroof		stryven
stynte, ('cease')	stynte,		stynted
stente	stente		stynt, stent
swelle	swal		swollen
swelte ('die', 'faint')	swelte		
swere	swo(o)r	swore	swore
swymme		swommen	
swynke ('toil')			swonke
synge	sang, so(o)ng	songe	songe
synke	sank		sonke
take	took	tooke	take
teche	taughte		taught
telle	tolde		toold
thenche see *thynke*			
thenke see *thynke*			
throwe	threw		throwe
thynke, thenche, thenke	thoughte		thought
trede	trad	troden	troden

INFINITIVE	PAST SG.	PAST PL.	PAST PART.
wake	waked, wo(o)k		waked, wakened
walke	walked, welk		walked
wasshe	wessh	wesshe	wasshe
waxe, wexe	wexe, we(e)x, wax	wexe, woxe	waxe, woxe
wende ('go')	wente		went
wepe	wepte, we(e)p		wept, wopen, wepen
werke, ('work') werche, wirche	wroughte		wrought
weve ('weave')	waf		woven
wexe see *waxe*			
wil see *wol*			
wirche see *werke*			
wol, ('will') wil	wolde		wold
wreke ('avenge')	wrak		wreke, wroken
write	wroot	writen	writen
wynne	wan		wonne
yelde ('yield')	yald		yolden
yeve, yive	yaf	yave	yeve, yive.

Select Bibliography

This bibliography is chiefly limited to some of the most important book length works on Chaucer's language. A few articles have, however, been included; some because they are of special importance, others because they are concerned with specific problems discussed in this book.

For more detailed bibliographical information the reader is referred to standard bibliographies such as George Watson (ed.) *The New Cambridge Bibliography of English Language and Literature*, Vol. I, Cambridge, 1974; the *Annual Bibliography of English Language and Literature*; *The Year's Work in English Studies*. There are also specialised Chaucer bibliographies such as D. D. Griffith, *Bibliography of Chaucer 1908–53*, Seattle, 1955; W. R. Crawford, *Bibliography of Chaucer 1954–63*, Seattle and London, 1967, Lorrayne Y. Baird, *A Bibliography of Chaucer 1964–73*, Boston, Mass., 1977.

Burnley, J. D., *Chaucer's Language and the Philosophers' Tradition*, Cambridge, 1979.
Burnley, J. D., *A Guide to Chaucer's Language*, London, 1983.
Burnley, J. D., 'Inflection in Chaucer's Adjectives', *Neuphilologische Mitteilungen*, LXXXIII (1982), 169–77.
Davis, Norman, 'Chaucer and Fourteenth-Century English', in *Writers and their Background: Geoffrey Chaucer*, ed. by D. S. Brewer, London, 1974, pp. 58–84.
Donaldson, E. Talbot, 'Chaucer's Final -*e*', *Publications of the Modern Language Association of America*, 63 (1948), 1101–24, and 64 (1949), 609.
Eliason, Norman E., *The Language of Chaucer's Poetry: An Appraisal of the Verse, Style and Structure*, Anglistica 17, Copenhagen, 1972.
Elliott, Ralph W. V., *Chaucer's English*, London, 1974.
Fisiak, Jacek, *The Morphemic Structure of Chaucer's English*, Alabama Linguistic and Philological Series, 10, Alabama, 1965.
Karpf, Fritz, *Studien zur Syntax in den Werken Geoffrey Chaucers*, Vienna, 1930.
Kenyon, John S., *The Syntax of the Infinitive in Chaucer*, London, 1909.
Kerkhof, J., *Studies in the Language of Geoffrey Chaucer*, Second, revised and enlarged edition, Leyden, 1982.
Kökeritz, Helge, *A Guide to Chaucer's Pronunciation*, New Haven, Conn., 1954.
Langhans, Viktor, 'Der Reimvokal *e* bei Chaucer', *Anglia*, 45 (1921), 221–82, 297–392.
Masui, Michio, *The Structure of Chaucer's Rime Words: An Exploration into the Poetic Language of Chaucer*, Tokyo, 1964.

McJimsey, Ruth B., *Chaucer's Irregular -e*, New York, 1942.

Moore, Samuel, *Historical Outlines of English Sounds and Inflections*, revised by Albert Markwardt, Ann Arbor, 1951. Chapter 4.

Peters, R. A., *Chaucer's Language*, Journal of English Linguistics Occasional Monographs, I, Bellingham, Wash., 1980.

Roscow, Gregory, *Syntax and Style in Chaucer's Poetry*, Cambridge, 1981.

Samuels, M. L., 'Chaucerian Final -"E"', *Notes & Queries New Series*, 19 (1972), 445–48.

Schlauch, Margaret, 'Chaucer's Colloquial English: Its Structural Traits', *Publications of the Modern Language Association of America*, 67 (1952), 1103–16.

Southworth, James G., 'Chaucer's Final -e in Rhyme', *Publications of the Modern Language Association of America*, 62 (1947), 910–35, and 64 (1949), 601–10.

Spearing, A. C., 'Chaucer's Language', in *An Introduction to Chaucer*, ed. by M. Hussey, A. C. Spearing, and J. Winny, Cambridge, 1965, pp. 89–114.

Storms, G., 'A Note on Chaucer's Pronunciation of French *u*', *English Studies*, 41 (1960), 305–8.

Ten Brink, Bernhard, *The Language and Metre of Chaucer*, translated by M. B. Smith, London, 1901.

Wild, F. *Die sprachlichen Eigentümlichkeiten der wichtigeren Chaucer-Handschriften und die Sprache Chaucers*, Vienna, 1915.

Subject Index

Word Index

The index does not include words cited solely as examples of regular phonological, graphological, or morphological phenomena. In addition to 'words' proper the list includes prefixes (marked by a following hyphen) and suffixes (marked by a preceding hyphen).

The index is in strict alphabetical order, except that letters in brackets have been disregarded. Readers should therefore bear in mind what has been said about spelling variation in Chaucerian English. See remarks prefixed to the alphabetical list of irregular verbs p. 86.

a- 36, 37
abeye 70
aboght 70
abood 72
abought 70
aboughte 70
abreyde 77
abyde 72
abyden 72
abye 70
-age 35
alder 51
alight 76
alighte 76
aller 51
also 23
am 77
an- 37
answerd 78
answerde 78
answere 78
answered 78
ar(e) 77
arisen 72
arist 85

arn 77
aroos 72
arryve 66
art 77
aryse 72
aryseth 85
assaye 66
astert 79
asterte 79
asterted 79
-atif 40
atteyne 69
atteynt 69
-atyf 40
awake 79
awaked 79
awo(o)k 79
awreke 73
awroken 73
baar 73
bad 74
bake 74
bar 73
bare 73
bee *n.* 45

be(e) *v.* 21, 77
beautee 27
bed 49
bede 74
been 21, 77
beer 73
beete 74
behelde 75
behette 76
ben 77
bende 70
bent 70
bente 70
bere 73
beren 73
beryis 44
best 55
bet 56
bete 22, 74
beth 77
bette 74
bettre 55, 56
beye 70
bidde 74
bifalle 75

halt 4, 84
han 69
hange 79
hanged 79
hatte 76
have 68
he 21, 57
he(e)d *n.* 21
-hed 40
heelp 74
heeng 79
heet 76
heete 76
hef 74
held 75
helde 75
helpe 74
hem 57, 59
hemself, -selve(n) 63
heng 79
hent 76
hente 76
herd 67
herde 67
here *v.* 67
here *pron.* 57, 59, 60
herte *v.* 76
het 76
heve 74
hidden 68
hight 76
highte 76
him 57
himselve 63
hir(e) 57, 59, 60
hires 57, 59
hirs 57
hirself, -selve(n) 63
his 57, 59
hit 57
-hod 40
holde 75, 85
holdeth 4, 84, 85
holpe 74
hond(e) 50
honge 79
hoot *adj.* 55
hoote *v.* 76
hors 46
hose 45
hote *v.* 76
hotter 55
hottest 55
hous 47
hurt 76

hurte 76
hyd 67, 68
hydde 67, 68
hyde 67, 68
hymself, -selve(n) 63
hyndreste 57
I 57
i- 36–37, 64
ich 57, 59
-if 40
is 77
ispendid 78
it 57
its 59
itself 63
joye 9
karf 73
kene 52
kepe 78
keped 78
kept 78
kepte 78
kerve 73
kidde 78
kist 78
kiste 78
kithe 78
kithed 78
kitte 79
knew(e) 74
knowe 74
knyf 47
knyt 76
knytte 76
korve 73
kyd 78
kysse 78
kyssed 78
lad 68
ladde 68
lady 47, 49
laft 69
lafte 69
lasse 55
last 55
laste 79
lasted 79
late 55
latter 55
laughe 79
laughed 79
laughen 79
laxatyf, -yves 47
lay(e) 75
led 68

ledde 68
lede 68
leef *n.* 47
leep 77
leest 55
leet 74
leete 74
left 69
lefte 69
lene 69
lenger 55
lengest 55
lent 69
lente 69
lepe 77
les 80
lese 80
lesse 55
lete 74
leve 69
levere 55
levest 55
lewed 27
leyd 67
leyde 67
leye 67
leyn 75
-lich(e) 40
lief 55
lif 47
ligge 75
liken 60
liste 76
lond(e) 50
long 55
longer 55
lore 80
lorn 80
lost 80
loste 80
lough 79
love 83–85
-ly 40, 57
lye 75
lytel 55
lyven 72
maad 78
made 78
make 78
maked 78
malt 73
man 45, 49
many 55
may 81
mayst 81

me 21, 57
meeke 52
melte 73
mene 78
mened 78
ment 78
mente 78
met 71
me(e)te 21, 22, 71
mette 71
mo(o) 55
molte 73
moon 11, 12
moore 55
more *n.* 24
moost *adj.* 55
moot(e) 81
mooten 81
most(e) *v.* 81
mosten 81
mote 81
mous 45
mowe(n) 81
muche(l) 55
murierly 57
my 57, 58, 59
myghte 81
myn(e) 57, 58, 59, 60
myself, -selve(n) 63
-n 64, 65, 66, 85
nadde 69
nam 77
nart 77
nas 77
nath 69
neet 46
nere 77
-nesse 40
nether 57
nis 77
nolde 69
noot 83
nost 83
not 83
nyl 69
nylt 69
nys 77
nyste 83
of- 37
oghte(n) 81, 82
oghtest 81
old 42, 55
on- 37
ooth 47
oughte(n) 81, 82

oughtest 81
our(e) 57, 59, 60
oures 57, 59
overeste 57
owe 81, 82
owed 81, 82
owen 81, 82
owest 81, 82
oweth 81, 82
oxe 44
passe 78
passed 78
past 78
paste 78
payd 78
payde 78
paye 78
payed 78
pleyd 67
pleyde 67
pleye 67
plight 77
plighte 77
pound 46
presse 78
pressed 78
prest 78
preyde 78
preye 78
preyed 78
put 77
putte 77
quake 79
quaked 79
quenche 70
queynt 70
queynte 70
quit 71
quite 71
quitte 71
quo(o)k 79
rad 68
radde 68
raft 69
rafte 69
ran 73
raughte 70
recche 70
reche 70
red *v.* 68
red *adj.* 21, 55
redde 68
redder 55
rede *v.* 68
reed *adj.* 21, 55

reft 69
refte 69
reighte 70
rekke 70
rende 70
renne 73
rent 70
rente 70
reve 69
riden 72
rideth 84
risen 72
rist 85
rit 84
rong 72
ronge 72
ronne 73
rood 72
roos 72
roughte 70
ryde 72
rynge 72
ryse 72
ryseth 85
-s 43–44, 46, 48
sang 72
sank 72
sat 75
sate 75
saugh(e) 4, 75
save 66
saw(e) 4, 75
sawgh 4, 75
say(e) 4, 75
sched 68
se(e) *n.* 22
se(e) *v.* 4, 75
seche 70
seeth 76
seigh 4, 75
seke *v.* 21, 70
-self, -selve(n) 62–63
selle 67
sende 70
sene 75
sent 70
sente 70
set 76
sete 75
seten 75
sethe 76
sette 76
sey(n) *v.* 83–85
seyd 67
seyde 67

seye 67
seyn 75
shad 68
shadde 68
shake 74
shal 82
shalt 82
shape 74
she 21, 57
shedde 68
shede 68
sheep 46
shende 70
shent 70
shente 70
shet 77
shette 77
shewe 27
ship(e) 48, 50
sho 23, 47
sholde 82
shon v. 79
shook 74
shoon 79
shoop 74
shope 74
shryven 72
shul(le) 82
shyne 79
shyned 79
shynen 79
sigh 4, 75
sighte 79
sike 79
siked 79
sitte 75
slawe 75
slayn 75
slee 75
sleep 80
slepe 80
slepte 80
slough 75
slow(e) 75
smoot 72
smyte 72
smyten 72
so(o) 23
sode 76
solde 67
-som 40
song 71, 72
songe 71, 72
sonke 72
soold 67

soon 11, 12, 23
soong 71, 72
sought 70
soughte 70
sowe ('sow') 74
spak 74
spake 74
span 72
sped 67
spedde 67
spe(e)de v. 21, 67
speke 74
spende 78
spent 78
spente 78
spille 69
spilt 69
spoke 74
sponne 72
sprad 68
spradde 68
sprang 72
sprede 68
sprong 72
spronge 72
sprynge 72
spynne 72
-st verbal suffix 84
-st superlative 54
staf 47
stal 73
stant 85
starf 73
stele 73
stent 79
stente 79
stepe 22
-stere 35, 40
stert 77
sterte 77
sterve 73
stode 75
stole 73
stonde 75
stondeth 85
stood 75
stoon 11, 12, 24
storve 73
straught 79
straughte 79
strecche 79
strecched 79
streighte 79
strenger 55
strengest 55

strete 22
streyght 79
strong 55
stroof 72
stryve 72
stryven 72
stynt 79
stynte 79
stynted 79
suster 45
swal 73
sweete adj. 52
swelle 73
swelte 77
swere 74
swete v. 22
swollen 73
swommen 72
swonke 72
swo(o)r 74
swore 74
swymme 72
swyn 46
swynke 72
sy 4, 75
syen 75
synge 71, 72, 84–85
synke 72
take 74
taught 70
taughte 70
teche 70
telle 67
-th 85
thair 59
that 62
the(e) 57, 59
theef 47
thenche 70
thenke 70
there 28
thes 62
these 62
the which(e) 62
they 57
thing 46
this 62
thise 62
tho 62
thou 57, 59
thought 70
thoughte 70
thow 57, 59
threw 74
throwe 74

106

thy 57, 58, 59
thyn(e) 57, 58, 59
thynke 70
thyself, -selve(n) 63
tolde 67
to *prep.* 23
to- 37
too *n.* 45
took(e) 74
toold 67
tooth 45
-tou, -tow (= 'thou') 60
town(e) 50
trad 73
trede 73
trewe 52
troden 73
Troye 9
us 57
us self, -selve(n) 63
vers 46
waf 73
wake 79
waked 79
wakened 79
walke 79
walked 79
wan 72
-ward 35, 41
was 77
wasshe 75
wax(e) 75
we 21, 57
weep 80
weex 75
wel 56
welk 79
wende 70, 75
went 70
wente 70, 75
wep 80
wepe 80
wepen 80
wept 80

wepte 80
werche 70
were 28, 77
weren 28, 77
werke 70
werse 55
werst 55
wessh 75
wesshe 75
weve 73
wex(e) 75
where 28
which(e) 61–62
white 55
whitter 55
who 61
whom 61
whos 61
whoso 61
wif 47
wil 69
wilde 52
wilt 69
wirche 70
wist 83
wiste 83
wite 83
witen 83
wo 23
wok 79
wol 14, 69
wold 69
wolde 69
woldest 69
wole 69
wolt 69
woman 45, 49, 50
wonne 72
wook 79
woost 83
woot 83
wopen 80
word 14

world 14
worm 14
worse 55
worst 55
wortes 14
worthy 14
wost 83
wot 83
woven 73
woxe 75
wrak 73
wreke 73
write 72
writen 72
wroken 73
wroot 72
wrought 70
wroughte 70
wynne 72
wynter 46
wyve 72
y- 36–37, 64
yaf 74
yald 73
yave 74
ye(e) 57, 60
yede 75
yeer(e) 46, 50
yelde 73
yer(e) 46, 50
yeve 74
-yf 40
yfled 80
yive 74
yiven 72
yolden 73
you 57
your(e) 57, 59, 60
youres 57, 59
youreself, -selve(n) 63
yow 57, 60
yspred 68
yvel 55